WIN WITH LYNNE

Simply Slogans

Lynne Suzanne

Other book by the same author:

Win With Lynne
How To Win Consumer Competitions

WIN WITH LYNNE

Simply Slogans

Lynne Suzanne

L A Design Books

First published in Great Britain by:

L A Design Books
PO Box 11
Skegness
PE25 3QH
Lincolnshire

Copyright © 1996 Lynne Suzanne

ISBN 0 9151011 4 3

All rights reserved; no part of this publication may be reproduced, stored in a retrieval system, or transmitted by any form or by any means, electronic, mechanical, photocopying, recording or otherwise, without the prior written permission of the Publishers.

British Library Cataloguing-in-Publication Data:

A catalogue record of this book is available from the British Library

Drawings: D. D.
Photography: Bob Turner
　　　　　　　D. Charles

Printed and bound by:
Mastin Print, Skegness, Lincs.

Greet your postman with a grin
Learn the secrets, Win With Lynne

Win With Lynne - Simply Slogans, Lynne's second book, is inspired by her popular *Simply Slogans* weekend course and based on her own successful winning methods.

CONTENTS

		Page
Introduction		3
Chapter One	Steps to Success	5
Chapter Two	Intaslogans	11
Chapter Three	Words of Phrase	21
Chapter Four	On the Write Lines	23
Chapter Five	Intaslogans Winning Ways	27
Chapter Six	Personally Speaking	29
Chapter Seven	Styles of Slogans	43
Chapter Eight	Simply Slogans	48
Chapter Nine	Prizewinning Slogans	70
Chapter Ten	Lynspiration	87
Index		98
Lynformation Pack		100

INTRODUCTION

Win With Lynne
Simply Slogans

WIN WITH LYNNE - Simply Slogans has been written especially for people who enjoy the fun and challenge of entering a variety of consumer competitions, ranging from free draws, researching tasks and especially those involving writing a tiebreaker slogan.

As compers, you may be aware of the maxim 'easy to enter, hard to win', which is certainly true when it comes to competitions. Your chances of winning free to enter, 'first out of the hat' draws are far less than for those contests requiring skill. Your greatest chance of success lies in those contests which involve writing a tiebreaker slogan. The majority of the consumer competitions in the UK today, consist of a two-part contest. The first part normally involves skill, for example: answering factual questions, a wordsearch, rearranging anagrams etc. The second part is the tiebreaker, which usually calls for the completion of a sentence.

So having completed the first part of the contest satisfactorily, confident the answers are correct, and therefore, knowing your tiebreaker will reach the judging stage, what then? More experienced compers will be aware it pays to write, polish and perfect a tiebreaker, if it is to make it to the final judging and prize awarding session.

Many beginners, myself included, when first discovering competitions, are often under the impression, having completed the first part of the task, that the tiebreaker doesn't particularly matter. They mistakenly think this will only be used as a last resort, should a handful of entrants arrive at this stage. It comes then, as a complete eye-opener to realise thousands of people enter competitions. Should the first part of the task consist of easy questions, then thousands of people will make it through to the judging session. Once the significance of this is realised, closer attention is given to the tiebreaker slogan.

I appeared on Granada Television's 'This Morning' to talk about my favourite hobby, and the launch of my first comping book *Win With Lynne - How to Win Consumer Competitions*. During the show, viewers were invited to enter a telephone competition, which involved submitting a limerick. I, and another well-known comper, was asked to judge this competition and it gave me an opportunity to look at tiebreakers from a different viewpoint, i.e. that of a judge. Telephone staff wrote the tiebreakers down and passed them to us for judging. Speed was of the essence, as we had to find two winners and report back to the studio in a short space of time. Thus, each tiebreaker received only a quick glance, before being put on the 'reject' or the 'worthy of further consideration' pile. You can appreciate then, after looking through hundreds of similar sounding phrases, it was easy to spot those with eye-catching words. A useful lesson to learn is never under-estimate the opposition.

After writing a tiebreaker, I always leave it for a couple of days, then come back to it with fresh eyes, viewing it as though I were a judge, reading it quickly and mentally placing it on the 'reject' or 'worthy of further consideration pile'.

So just why is it top compers are consistent winners? Pure luck ! There has to be an element of luck, in that entrants do not know what the judges are looking for. What one judge likes, another doesn't. In the main, winning depends on skill, perseverance, practice and patience, coupled with a positive and optimistic outlook. Entering competitions is a fun, fascinating and challenging hobby. And as a bonus, I've made so many wonderful new friends too.

How then, do you acquire this skill? By looking, listening and learning. Looking at promoters advertisements so your tiebreakers are written on the 'write lines'. Listening to advice and hints from other compers, and trying out new styles of writing. Learning, by studying the winners lists and noting the styles favoured by the various promoters, then comparing these with your own submissions. The only tools you need are words. They just need to be the 'write' words, written in an apt, original and eye-catching way.

The aim of *Win With Lynne - Simply Slogans*, is quite simply to provide you with inspiration, hints and advice to writing winning tiebreakers. We all dream of receiving long white envelopes, congratulating us on winning an exotic holiday, a luxurious cruise or a brand new car.

In my first year of comping, I won only small prizes, video tapes, tee-shirts etc. I then spent a year researching the topic and learning how to write winning tiebreakers. After my 'apprenticeship' my first 'biggie' was a holiday in Devon, followed by a television, video recorder and wardrobe of clothes. Then I won my first car, a Ford Fiesta, which was first prize in a tiebreaker competition. Two years later I won my second car, a Proton Persona, in a national competition. I have won hundreds of smaller prizes and been on holiday in the UK, Amsterdam, Spain, the Bahamas, Miami, the Gulf of Mexico, Isla de Margarita and Venezuela.

Win With Lynne - Simply Slogans, reveals my secrets of success and is based on my popular *Simply Slogan* weekend courses. Together we look at brainstorming, constructing tiebreakers, and the effective use of *Intaslogans* wordbanks to polish and perfect our finished tiebreaker slogans. We also look at different styles of slogans, so you can vary entries and increase your chances of winning. Plus of course, some light-hearted reading along the way.

Some compers like to read a book, others like to be shown how to write tiebreakers and would find the annual *Simply Slogans* weekend inspirational. Most people I've met, just love to meet other like-minded compers to chat about their favourite hobby, swap entry forms and share tips and hints. *Intacomps* social days, provide a perfect opportunity to do this and are now held regularly throughout the UK.

Competitions are a fun, enjoyable, challenging, stimulating and exciting hobby. They may even change your lifestyle - mine did.

Wishing you every success with your future entries,
Best Wishes

CHAPTER ONE
Steps to Success

Many compers will be aware that writing winning tiebreakers requires skill. Most of these consist of a two-part task. The first part is normally answering factual questions, completion of a wordsquare, rearranging anagrams or similar. The second part is the tiebreaker stage. The easier the first part of the task, the more entrants will have the correct solution, and therefore more entries will reach the judging of the tiebreaker.

From the moment competition entries are opened, a process of elimination begins until the first prize winner is chosen. Firstly, any entries arriving after the closing date will be disqualified. Next the envelope will be opened and the entry coupon and qualifier removed. The qualifier may be a till receipt, bar code or whatever item you have been asked to include to qualify for entry. Any entries without the qualifier are eliminated. Similarly, each entry remaining will be checked to ascertain the solution to the first part of the task is correct, resulting in more eliminations. Can the judges read your writing? Illegible entries and those with crossings out and smudged writing also hit the waste paper basket. Different judging panels will have their own criteria to work to, as the mammoth task of judging the final part of the task, i.e. the tiebreaker, begins. Eventually, they will be left with a number of good entries, the winner and runners-up decided and the prizes awarded.

When is a Slogan not a Slogan

So just what is a tiebreaker? A tiebreaker decides who shall win the prize. Reading through a selection of entry forms, this can take the form of an estimation, for example: how many miles from London to Paris; the naming of an airliner; a caption for a cartoon, but more often a sentence completion or slogan is required. For the purpose of this book, I will use the term 'tiebreaker' to mean either a slogan or sentence completion. A slogan is a sentence or phrase which is complete in its own right, for example, the famous slogan:

Beanz Meanz Heinz

A sentence completion is where the entrant is asked to complete a sentence for a given lead-in line, for example:

I buy my beans from Lynne's store because...
They're open till late, with no check out wait

There is a tendency, when sitting alone at the dining room table, working on these sentence completions, to think you are the only person entering. You tend to forget about the thousands of other entrants, similarly sitting at their tables, working away. Writing winning tiebreakers is not easy. It requires skill. Take heart though, this skill can be learned.

Four Steps to Success

When you are ready to commence writing your tiebreakers, it is advisable to deal with each competition entry form in turn. Make a study of it, read the instructions carefully and observe the competition rules. Note the closing date, which is the latest date entries must be received at the competition address. Then on a blank sheet of paper, write down the lead-in line, for example:

I buy Brand X cheese at Lynne's store because...

Look at the entry form for clues. It may say 'complete the tiebreaker sentence in not more than 12 words in an apt and amusing manner', so to produce a serious sentence will be a waste of time and postage. Similarly, your entry will hit the waste paper basket should you exceed the word limit. It is advisable to count words such as "they're" and "you'll" as two separate words. Do study the image of the promoter. Look at the message they are putting across to you, the consumer. Ask yourself questions: is it a new product to their existing range, or an old favourite which has been relaunched with new packaging. Maybe it's a new company and you need to know what the product does and who it's aimed at.

Marketing plays a large part in selling products and the entrant should be aware of the promoters image. Take soap powder as an example. You would imagine that most people use this product, therefore the manufacturers would aim their marketing at everyone. Not so. You have only to look at the range of soap powders on the supermarket shelves to notice there are several brands aimed at different groups of consumers. For example: young mums, who need to know a particular powder will remove food, grass and rough and tumble dirt stains from their youngsters clothes, through to the colour fashion conscious, who want to be assured their soap powder will not fade their bright reds to pale pink.

It pays to praise the promoter, to find positive statements to write about their products. A word of warning though, don't overdo it so it becomes untrue or wildly exaggerated. It is also advisable to study the theme of the contest, for example: if it is about Italy, with a trip to Rome as the prize and the product is Italian sauce, then do give your tiebreaker an Italian slant. Study individual advertising slogans in magazines, literature and on television and notice if they are amusing, sincere, written in rhyme and how many words they contain. You'll soon get the idea.

When I finally post my tiebreakers, I will have worked through four steps before arriving at the end result. These are: brainstorming, constructing phrases, completing the tiebreaker and perfecting the tiebreaker.

Step One - Brainstorming

Brainstorming simply means writing down all thoughts that come into your head which have relevance to the task in hand. It is usually at this stage, compers sit with a pen in one hand, and think, where do I start, my mind's gone a blank. Sounds familiar !

Chapter One: Steps to Success

It is much easier to build up a tiebreaker when you have a starting point. Brainstorming will provide you with both words and inspiration. To commence, I suggest you take a blank sheet of paper and at the top, write down the lead-in line, underlining any keywords, for example:

I buy my <u>Italian sauce</u> from <u>Lynne's store</u> because...

Next, draw four vertical columns with the headings:

<u>Product</u>   <u>Store</u>   <u>Theme</u>   <u>Prize</u>

Now, commencing with the first column, ask yourself questions such as: why do I buy this brand of sauce, rather than any other make? And no, not because you wanted to enter the competition! Even if it is true! Now write down your thoughts under product, for example:

<u>Product</u>
good selection
wide range of flavours
choice of spicy or extra spicy
tangy taste
quick and easy
made in minutes
generous servings

Ma - car - oni, exciting twist, for delicious re - sauce - ful dish

Moving on to the store, ask yourself questions such as, why do I shop at Lynne's store rather than anywhere else? Write down your thoughts, for example:

Shopped elsewhere but couldn't budg - et !

<u>Store</u>
friendly staff
conveniently located
ample car parking
open late
stocks my favourite brand names
competitive prices
customer service

When you come to a stop, which you will at some point, move on to the next column. In many cases you will find the prize reflects the theme of the competition. For example: an Italian sauce with a prize holiday to Italy.

<u>Prize</u>   <u>Theme</u>
Italy
have a leaning for Pisa / pizza
towering above
pasta-port, pasta my expectations
Rome around
canna - letto myself
it cannelloni be a

I've a leaning for a pizza !

For a competition featuring a new fun product, for example: dinosaur shaped pasta with a prize family holiday to Disneyland, clearly the Prize section would be based on Disneyland. The theme would be about fun, laughter and enjoyment. Once a flow of words start, you will find yourself moving back and forth from one column to the next. Before long, you'll have a page full of words and ideas to work from.

The purpose of a brainstorming session is to get you thinking and putting thoughts to paper, regardless of whether those thoughts and words have any relevance to your final tiebreaker. This is much better than leaning with your elbows on the table, pen in mouth, studying a blank sheet of paper, and thinking 'where do I start'? The more ideas and words you have to choose from, the easier it will become to write your tiebreaker. The time to stop writing and move onto the next step is as soon an idea strikes you. And it will !

The purpose of writing your ideas and words in headed columns is two-fold. Firstly, upon reading the completed lists you may notice a word or phrase has been repeated in more than one column. Perhaps you'd like to use this selling point or key feature as the central idea for your tiebreaker. Sometimes a word has a double meaning and can be used to good effect in an eye-catching tiebreaker, using play on words, for example: Rome - roam. The second reason for writing your ideas and words in columns is to commence building a wordbank. When I began entering competitions I would brainstorm the product, then construct phrases and finally write the tiebreaker. I would then throw away my notes. The next time a similar contest came along, I would commence the whole brainstorming process again.

Then it occurred to me those previous lists would come in useful, so then I started my wordbank. This has proved so useful as I not only save time, but I have at hand a whole wealth of words. If I were asked to name my most important tools for comping, these would be my wordbank and rhyming dictionary. In chapter two, I share extracts from my own wordbank with you, aptly entitled *Intaslogans*.

Step Two - Constructing Phrases

Having made a list of suitable words and phrases under the four column headings, you are now ready to move on to step two, stringing the words and phrases into longer phrases. You may find as you look down your word lists, a particular word will trigger off an idea and you can then begin to make a phrase. On occasions this does not happen. So do try asking yourself questions. Write down your answer in a simple statement, giving no particular thought to your choice of words, for example: does this Italian sauce have any special selling point or ingredient, which its rivals do not have? Yes, you may answer: it comes in convenient jars, and I love its unique tangy tomato flavour. Now although not the most brilliant of statements, it is a starting point and your opinion as a consumer is invaluable.

Tiebreakers can be written in several different ways, for example: one-line statements, two-line rhyming couplets etc. You may decide to write your tiebreaker using a two-line rhyming couplet and would like to have a play on words. Do look through your brainstorming lists to find any words with double meanings for example: Rome - roam.

Chapter One: Steps to Success

The use of puns and word play is an effective way of making tiebreakers eye-catching. You may like to make use of a rhyming dictionary, to find suitable rhyme endings, for example: flavour - savour. This may then give you an idea for a phrase, for example:

This unique flavour is the taste to savour

Step Three - Completing Tiebreakers

The third step is where you combine your phrases, chopping and changing words here and there, to finish up with, hopefully, a winning tiebreaker. For example, in a cookery contest with a holiday prize to India on offer, you may have written a two-line rhyming couplet:

Gorgeous flavours, taste supreme
Indian holiday, exciting dream

You may then decide to go through the word lists again and have another attempt to see if you can better this one. Alternatively, you may decide you like this and post it off straight away. The choice is yours.

At a comping event, this subject came up in conversation. I said I always put my tiebreakers on one side and return to them a few days later, with fresh eyes. Sometimes, I felt I couldn't improve on it and would then post it. Whilst more often, I would find a more apt word which could be substituted, thereby improving my tiebreaker. On other occasions, I've thought 'what a load of rubbish' and consequently consigned it to the waste paper basket, and started again. A comping friend from the Midlands, who is very successful, having won many exotic holidays, says she always writes her tiebreakers, then pops them straight into envelopes and posts them. It really doesn't matter which method you use, the aim is merely to give you different ideas, from which you can take or leave or adapt as you wish.

Step Four - Perfecting Tiebreakers

Assuming you have decided to leave your tiebreaker and return to it with fresh eyes, let's have another look and see if this can be improved.

Gorgeous flavours, taste supreme
Indian holiday, exciting dream

You may feel you'd like to change a word, but nothing suitable springs to mind. This is where your list of brainstorming words will prove invaluable. Looking through these words under the heading of Travel - India, may reveal the word Goa. You could then change Gorgeous into GOA-geous, which not only uses a play on words but makes your tiebreaker more apt and eye-catching:

GOA-geous flavours, taste supreme
Indian holiday, exciting dream

Perfecting tiebreakers may mean the difference from no prize to a runners-up prize or a runners-up prize to a major prize. Consider: a tee-shirt or a gleaming new car !

There are many different ways to write tiebreakers, and should the rules allow multiple entries you may like to submit several tiebreakers, varying the styles used. One could be a simple one-line praise-the-product tiebreaker, another a two-line rhyming couplet perhaps using puns, whilst yet another uses alliteration or nostalgia.

Tiebreakers should sound pleasing to the ear and trip off the tongue. You will find lots of tips and hints to help you with writing tiebreakers in the following chapters, as we take a took at scansion, building and using effective wordbanks and styles of slogans.

There are also lists of homonyms and homophones for use in wordplay. Together with pages of tiebreaker ideas, listed in products and themes for easy reference. All designed to spark off ideas and help you produce your own original winning tiebreakers. Plus, of course, some light-hearted reading along the way.

From Beginner to Winner

Should you be a newcomer to comping, I am sure you will have found this chapter useful in explaining how writing winning tiebreakers can be broken down into four steps.

For the more experienced compers, I'm sure you will find the *Intaslogans* wordbanks, invaluable. Perhaps to use alongside your own records.

You will be able to see how these words and phrases appear as complete tiebreakers in *Prizewinning Slogans* chapter nine, and experiment with new and win-teresting styles.

Your appetite whetted ? Enthusiasm renewed ? Let's move on.

CHAPTER TWO

Intaslogans

Brainstorming

After brainstorming each individual competition, then completing and posting my tiebreaker, the word lists would be consigned to the waste paper basket, only to start the process all over again. I quickly realised I was wasting time and effort repeating brainstorming sessions, and set about building my *Intaslogans* wordbank.

The next time I brainstormed a competition, I neatly copied out the words onto separate sheets of A4 loose leaf papers, one sheet each for the product, store, prize and theme. Sometimes, when the prize and theme were similar, words from both columns would be listed on one sheet of paper, for example: prize holiday to Disneyland, with a Disney theme, would all be listed under the heading of Disney.

These sheets of paper headed, for example: cheese, store, Disney are then filed alphabetically in A4 loose leaf folders. The next time a similar competition for cheese arises, I have a ready made list of suitable cheese words for inspiration. You may find the next cheese competition offers a prize holiday to Switzerland. It then becomes a simple matter to select both the cheese words from the products and Switzerland from the travel theme section.

My own *Intaslogans* wordbank has grown to fill several A4 loose leaf folders, which is divided into products and themes. It has become necessary to divide some of the headings into subheadings. Dairy products is sub-divided into cheese, butter, yoghurt, cream and milk. Similarly, my laundry file is sub-divided into fabric conditioners, soap powder, washing machines and tumble dryers.

I make a point of continually adding to my wordbank. Words and phrases are gleaned from a variety of sources, including my brainstorming sessions, watching television advertisements, listening to amusing snippets and jokes, noting eye-catching words from magazines and newspapers. Here is a selection taken from newspapers:

    shear attack
    first and floormost
    motorvation
    tan-tastic time
    you Kent beat the scenery
    best fruit forward

Many compers like to send for winners lists. You will find details of how to obtain these in the rules on individual entry forms. Alternatively, you will find tiebreakers in the series of *Prizewinning Slogans* booklets, more details in chapter nine.

You may like to note the winning tiebreaker alongside your own entry. You do keep records of which ones you submitted, I hope? Then, when the promoter organises a similar competition, you will know the style of tiebreaker which was favoured. This can give you an edge on the competition. This is not to say however, just because a simple praise-the-product tiebreaker won last time, the same style will win again, but does serve as a useful guide-line.

You may find, should you be a beginner to comping, that looking at lists of words and phrases simply doesn't inspire you. You can't quite see how they will look in a finished tiebreaker. If so, you may like to ignore the rest of this chapter for the moment. However, I'm sure by the time you've reached the end of chapter five, you will be turning back and viewing these words with a new enthusiasm.

With *Intaslogans* wordbank, when you commence writing your next tiebreaker, all you need do is look up the relevant product, store and theme words. These will provide you with the inspiration you need to build up your tiebreakers. I'm sure you will agree this is a much better method than sitting with a pen in one hand, a blank sheet of paper and a blank 'where do I start' expression! Yes, I've had those moments too !

Intaslogans

My *Intaslogans* wordbank has been launched as a series of 28 page handy A5 size booklets in products and themes. The main part of each booklet contains tiebreakers, with just a small section of words and phrases, as I've found many compers prefer to look through complete tiebreakers for inspiration. *Intaslogans : Drinks,* has tiebreaker ideas on general drinks, coffee, tea, mineral water, soft drinks, beer, lager, wines and spirits. *Intaslogans : Dairy*, has ideas on cheese, butter and spreads, cream, milk and yoghurt. *Intaslogans : Sport* has ideas on cycling, football, golf, horse racing, motor racing, skiing, tennis, etc. An up-to-date list of *Intaslogans* booklets can be obtained; please see page 100 for details.

Chapter Two : Intaslogans

BABYCARE

Babyfood, nappies, etc

- affection
- babies changing needs
- babies steal the show
- baby grows
- beats the rest
- best
- better than mine
- bottom
- bottom on prices
- building blocks
- carefully balanced
- carefully blended
- carefully selected
- changing needs
- changing years
- convenient jars
- convenient sizes
- cot
- crib
- delicious
- delightful
- drying up
- dryness
- dummies
- expertly blended
- feeding perfection
- flavour
- fuller flavour
- goodness
- growing needs
- grown-up menus
- gurgling
- handy little pots
- happy days
- healthy and happy
- healthy baby
- here to maternity
- home-made taste
- hungry tums
- ingredients
- keep baby dry
- keep baby clean
- leaks
- little darlings
- little jars
- little treasures
- love and affection
- maternity
- memories
- nappies
- nappiness
- natal attraction
- nature intended
- no waste
- nutritious ingredients
- off on the right foot
- pampering
- pram-tastic
- priceless on bottoms
- pure perfection
- purest ingredients
- safe without tears
- saves me time
- scampers
- scrumptious baby food
- selection
- smells sweet and fresh
- soak up the splash
- steal the show
- tasty meals
- tempt
- timesaving
- tiny tots
- toddlers
- top to bottom
- top to toe
- tops for bottoms
- tops for value
- tots to teens
- treasured possession
- trust
- varieties
- wholesome and pure
- younger generation

CLEANSERS

Detergents, bleaches, polishes, etc

- after dinner glint
- best solution
- beyond compare
- bleaching
- brilliant start
- brilliant finish
- bright and beautiful
- caring
- clean and relax
- clean and strong
- clean round the world
- clean away
- clean home
- clean up your act
- cleaning power
- cloudy lining
- combination
- complete protection
- consistent results
- convenience
- craftsmanship
- cuts prices
- cuts through grease
- dazzling
- dirt attacks
- effective and efficient
- excellent value
- fulfil housewife's need
- gentle action
- gentle on hands
- germs are lurking
- gleaming reputation
- gleaming results
- gleams come true
- goodbuy to germs
- great success
- has the edge
- housewife friendly
- hygenic
- impressive
- in a flash
- innovation
- kind on price
- kitchen sink drama
- lasting shine
- legend in its own grime
- light work
- make my 'spray'
- more cleaning power
- moves in ever 'degreasing' circles
- multi-cleansing
- names to trust
- on reflection
- outshines the rest
- partner in grime
- perfect measure
- performance
- power and the glory
- powerful on
- prime importance
- protection pledge
- quick off the mark
- range is far reaching
- reduce labour
- reflections speak louder than words
- removing marks
- quick
- retains perfection
- scene of the grime
- shine with ease
- smear campaign
- smells so fresh
- smooth on hands
- span is spick
- sparkling results
- special sheen
- spotlessly clean
- squirt worries dirt
- strength of Hercules
- thoroughly cleans
- time after time
- top names in my cabinet

CLOTHING

Fashion design etc

accessories
adventurous
apparel
appearance
array
attire
authentic
boutique
button up
can weather the
casual wear
catwalk
chic
children's casuals
city clothes
classic clothes
classic design
comfortable
complements
country casuals
creations
cut
cut for action
decked out
designer label
designer look
designer skill
dress up
dressed to thrill
durable
elegant
eye-catching
fashion
flair
flattery
garb
garments
geared up for
gene-ius / jeanius
girl about town
glamorous
glittering occasions
in gear
inspire compliments
kitting out kids
know where to go
label
lingerie
lurex
macho man
million dollar look
mini
new look
pleats
practical
quality
robe
slip into
sparkling occasions
star quality
steals the show
stocking up
style
stylish beyond compare
stylishly neat
suit-able for
suit any occasions
tailored
tailor-made
toddlers togs
togged out
top to toe
tots to teens
trendsetter
trendy
try on
unbeatable quality
uniform
unquestionable quality
up-to-the-minute
vogue
waterproof
weatherproof
wrap

CONFECTIONERY

Sweets, chocolates, chews, etc

assortment
bite size
bountiful
bounty of fun
boxed
candies
candy / sugar dandy
caramel
chew chew (train)
chews the best
chocaholics
chocolate attractions
chocolate factory
chocolates
choosy, chewsy
citrus
consolation
contentment
creamy
dainty
dairy cream
dark chocolate
delicious
dips into
dreamy
ee by gum
end a good meal
family favourites
fruity
fun treats
galaxy of gifts
gum
lasting flavour
lemon
lime
lollipop
magic
magic moments
mandarin
melting moments
mentholyptus
milky
minty
mmm mouthwatering
more-ish
mouthful
mouthwatering
nougat
nutty
orangy
packs of flavour
pick a packet
pick and mix
pick of the pack
'plane' chocolate
quality
rainbow selection
raspberry
romantic
selection box
sherbet
smooth
soft centres
spearmint
special pleasure
strawberry
sugar and spice
sugary
superior selection
sweet as honey
sweet escape
sweet - heart
sweet tooth
sweets
tastebud tempting
tingle on the tongue
tingling
toffee
tongue tingling
treat size
tropical
tubes of
unique
variety
worth a mint
wrapped up

Chapter Two : Intaslogans

COSMETICS

DRINKS

Skincare, make-up, deodorants etc

active	lasting touch
admiring glance	lovely all day
arm in arm	lower my guard
attractive	makes good scents
best friend	mildly perfumed
catch my drift	moisturize
chic	move close as I like
careful cleansing	naturally best
close proximity	nature intended
confidence	no sweat !
continental	none smell sweeter
continental	nose quickly knows
cool confidence	odour-whelming
cool and calm	others see difference
cool, collected and	panache
in command	perfumed delight
delicacy of perfumery	perspire
delicate fragrance	persuasion
dependable	pleasant call to arms
doesn't dry up cash	protective
effective protection	reassuring
endearment	refreshing perfume
everlasting freshness	relied on
extremely effective	rolled on
fatal attractions	scent-sational
feel the difference	selective
feminine allure	shower fresh
femininity	smell divine
flatters	sprays 'misty' for me
floral	squirt
formula to succeed	stands the test of time
fresh and sweet	steamy encounters
fresh hour after hour	subtle fragrance
gentle body protection	superior selection
gentle perfume	sweet smell of
girls best friend	success
glances	tried and tested
home and dry	turns ponging into
in the nicest 'scents'	longing
intimate moments	underarm pollution
keeps me cool	undercover agent
keeps me fresh	whiff of
lady's charm	winning formula

Alcoholic
Beer and lager

a multitude of tins
always wins
best brew
brand buyers
can after can
cheers winning way
class in a glass
consistent quality
cool and dark
defy competition
excellent taste
finest beer
flavour to savour
frothy
good cheer
good head
high glass
home inn-joyment
inn-signia for
instant pleasure
it's brew-tiful
leader of the pack
light refreshment
long life lager
murder another case
my first case
no drought about it
one over the eight
outglass the
perfect brew
plenty of body
raising glasses to
refreshing reviver
rhythm and booze
sip sip hooray
started so ale finish
swirled
tastefully canned
thirst class
thirst quenching
traditional
widget

Alcoholic
Wines and spirits

bright and bubbly
champagne
cheers
complements
connoisseur
cool and crisp
crisp combination
delicious tasting
dinner for two
dry
essential blend of
expertly blended
fruity flavour
grapes of distinction
heard on grapevine
label / best on table
label perfection
launched a
magnificent
medium
one swallow makes a
summer / a party
party goes with zing
perfect bouquet
popular
quality seal
robust
romance
savour the flavour
setting the seal
sparkling
sparkling sensation
special occasion
sun-drenched grapes
superior wine
sweet
tastes a treat
the toast is cheers
thirst class honours
uncorking a
undiluted pleasure
vin ordinaire

DRINKS

Non Alcoholic
Tea and coffee

after brandy
aromatic
arousing aroma
bags of taste
blend justifies beans
blended
breakfast coffee
contented cups
cup above the rest
delightful
filters through
freshly brewed
frothier
ground
handy packs
hot water
instant
keeps well for longer
leaves me grounds
leaves me refreshed
medium roast
no grounds for
percolate
piping hot
price of a pot
refillable
refreshing
reviving
rich aroma
richly roasted
rise and shine
save as you urn
sip of tea
soothing cuppa
suits to the ground
superior
swallows
tea
urned a rest
urned the best
vacuum packed
well packed

Non Alcoholic
Soft drinks

appeal
appetising
bottlenecks
bottles of
canned for pleasure
cans of flavour
challenge
clutching at straws
cola
diet
diluted
drink and drive
energy
fizzical
fizzy
flavour
fruity flavours
healthy
lemony
mineral
mouthwatering
natural
quenching
reviver
richer for pourer
ring pull
soft drinks
sparkling companions
squash
squashes opposition
sugar free
superb
tastes like juice
tasty
thirst aid
thirst choice
thirst class
thirst quencher
thirsting for
top of the pops
water lot of
zing

ELECTRICAL

Electrical Appliances
TV, video, satellite, fridge, freezer, iron etc

applicances
astra-nomical value
audio
beams across nation
best reception
beyond their time
bits and bytes
channel hopping
completes the picture
computes the
control panel
controls the
craftsmanship
dazzling
dependability
dishing up selections
down to earth
dynamic
ease of workload
easily cleaned
economy
efficient
electricity
elbow grease
excellence
expert-ease
fast forward
fine tuners / tuna's
frequency
future dimension
futuristic
galaxy of
gleaming
great deals
guaranteed reliance
heavenly prices
hi-tech
mobile
multimedia
needs no adjustment
network
no more chores

on line
perception
performance
picture
plugged into
precision
pride of place
programmed in
quality
receives great
reception
receptiveness
rental charges
remote control
repeats
replay
right wave length
science
screened to
selection
service
spacious
speakers
star reception
storage space
style
superb quality
surfing the Net
technology
time for leisure
touch button
tuned to
unsurpassed
value
viewing
viewing opportunity
vision
visual
visual perfection
watt ohms need
wizardry
workplace

Chapter Two : Intaslogans

FOOD

Bakery
Bread, biscuits, etc

baked to a
banquet
batches
beautiful baking
beginners / winners
better bakes
breakfast, lunch, etc.
butty
chef's special
complements
cookery
crispy outers
cuisine
culinary
delicacies
domestic science
easy to use
etiquette
fairy cakes
family favourites
flexible
freezer
gastronomic
go between
gourmet
grains of
gran used to make
half baked prices
highest quality
lean cuisine
light and tasty
like gran used to make
loaves
low fat
makes baking pleasure
microwaves
mixing
oven to table
perfect pastry
raised to perfection
scrumptious inners
sun rises in the yeast

Dairy
Butter, cheese etc

beyond compare
bite size
blending oil
buttery taste
cheese 'bored'
churned for
complements
crackers
cool
creamy
delicious blend
expertly blended
field fresh flavour
finest ingredients
flavour's supreme
golden goodness
goodness
has grate appeal
healthy nutrition
it's grate
lashings of luxury
less fat / low fat
makes it gorge-ous
meadow fresh
natural goodness
nutritious
quality never wavers
rich and creamy
rivals churn out
smooth
spreads from cold
spreads straight from the fridge
spreads with ease
tastes like butter
tastes of summer
sun
thickly spread
vegetable oil
watch my weight
wedge
wholesome

Fruit & Veg
Potatoes, apples etc

ap'peel'ing price
apple of my eye
best of the bunch
chips
crunchy
D'you'C (juicy)
deliciously crisp
family lunch
gourmet dinner
grapevine
great ex-spud-tations
healthy
instant meals
jackets
juicy
label
natural goodness
nothing added
nothing removed
orchard fresh
packed for perfection
perfect
picked to perfection
picked to please
plump
reach their prime
regal fare
snacks
soil their reputation
sun-drenched
sunsational
superb selection
sweet
table quality
taste a-peel
taste sublime
tastebud tempters
tree-mendous value
vitamin C
warmest sun
zest
zingy

Meat
Beef, lamb, pork etc

a second butcher's
all strings bright
bring home the bacon
crest on the label
deserves an oinkore
fillet
gammonteed quality
go the whole hog
good grilling
grr-eatings
ham it up
in its prime
joint honours
keeps us perky
knocks stuffing out
less frying
mighty meaty
miles per gammon
once fried never forgotten
perfect porkies
perfectly cured
pigs in the pink
porkers
porkfect
ready sliced
reared
reasons / seasons
rind
roasting
saddle back
sausage for all season
sizzle siz it all
sizzling combination
sliced
smile on your chops
streaks ahead of
taste divine
tender
traditional
versatile
whole hog

LAUNDRY

Washing powders, conditioners, etc

- advance technology
- all pegged out
- automatic choice
- automatic winner
- awash with
- banish washday blues
- bright and breezy
- bright white
- brilliantly clean
- challenge
- clean out pockets
- cleanest
- cleans up on
- clear action
- clothes
- colour fast
- concentrated
- condition
- convenient
- cool degrees
- country fresh
- dazzling
- detergents
- drying's a breeze
- easy to use
- effective
- efficient feature
- environmentally green
- ex-static
- feel
- fragrant
- fresh air
- freshness
- gentle
- glowing in the wind
- green
- grime
- heaven scent
- improved action
- in the pink
- incredibly soft
- ingrained dirt
- large family washes
- leaves no marks
- lightness
- loads of bargains
- luxury
- material things
- meadow sweet
- micro powered
- non iron
- outdoor feel
- outdoor fresh
- perfect
- price pegging
- programmed to
- put to the test
- quick on the mark
- rainy days
- reliable
- removes soil
- satisfaction
- sheets ahead
- shifts dirt
- showers
- smells sweet
- soft soap
- solution to
- sparkling clean
- spring freshness
- stain free
- static prices
- summer all year
- technology
- tough on dirt
- unblemished
- united in whiteness
- value on every line
- warmth
- washday a breeze
- washday blues
- weather it be
- whatever the whiteness
- whiter than white
- winning line

MOTORING

Cars, petrol, accessories, etc

- appearance
- automatic
- bonnets
- boots
- brakes
- brand new wheels
- breaks
- bumper to bumper
- car care
- car - is - ma
- car in front
- chequered flag
- city crawl
- classic
- clean getaway
- clutch
- cruising
- dashboard
- dealership
- distributor
- drive the best
- driven to
- driving force
- economical
- elegant
- exciting
- exquisite style
- exterior
- family size
- formula for
- formula in the wet
- formula one
- formula to succeed
- garage
- garage guidance
- geared up for
- give way
- gleaming
- going is smooth
- great distributor
- hatchback
- highly motor-vated
- hot wheels
- ignition
- impressive
- in gear
- in the lead
- interior
- junction
- king of the road
- luxurious
- manifold advantages
- mile after mile
- miles better than
- motor-vation
- motorway melee
- motorway miles
- no accident
- no opposition
- number one
- on the move
- overdrive functions
- passed the test
- peak performance
- powerful
- quality
- rally on
- re-lion on
- roadhog
- roadside assistance
- saloon
- second to none
- showroom
- solution to pollution
- spacious
- spaghetti junction
- sporty little number
- streets ahead
- stylish
- transition
- transport
- travels triumphantly
- ultimate pair
- versatile
- wheels / deals
- winning combination

Chapter Two : Intaslogans

SPORT

Cycling

avoid traffic jams
comfort
countryside
cycle - ogical
economical
energy
family fun
finish the route
flat out
handle bars
healthy
in tandem
mountainous
no fumes
no pollution
on the move
open air
outdoors
pedal power
recycled
right gear
saddle bag
spare tyre
speed
start to flag
the route to
traffic
trendy
trustworthy
two wheel drive
wheels
youthful thrill

Football

action
attraction
boots
celebration
cheers
crowd puller
dream team
eleven
fan - tastic
final result
footwork
half time
jackpot
man of the moment
match of the day
net
no match for
no substitute
our aim is
our goal is
penalties
perfectly scored
plays into extra time
premier position
premiership brand
replays
results
saves
score goals
seasoned
professional
shot
spectacular result
striking display
strikingly clear
thrilling match
to boot
united supporters
value their goal
World Cup
atmosphere

Golf

champion
competition
course
driver
gain on the swings
green
has the edge
hole in one
nineteenth hole
play a round
putt together
wedge
winner

Horse Racing

champion
classic races
clear the fence
competition
course
falls at the first fence
fast
favourites
first past the post
flat racing
furlong
horse
jumpers
steeplechasers
strong finish
top jockey
well backed

Motor Racing

brakes
championship
chequered flag
crash helmet
fast time
formula one
leaders
no indy - cisions
pit starts
pole position
second to none
seconds away
steer clear
winning formula

Olympic Events

all nations
amateur athletics
atmosphere
bronze, silver medals
decathlon
five rings
friendship
going for gold medal
peak performance
sensation
silver medals
sporting chance
standing ovation
top performance

Skiing

bruises, falls
going downhill
piste
slalom
snow risk of
summit it all up
to the top
we al-pine for

Snooker

on cue
pocket the
balls
colours
championship

Tennis

ace
court
grass
net
top of the game
championship
top seeded

TRAVEL - COUNTRIES

Africa and the Middle East

Anthony
asping for more
Cleopatra
Egyptian
Julius Caesar
Nile
sphinx

Asia and the Far East

eastern
great wall
oriental
saucery tricks
spicy
thai up
wok
yen to roam

Australia

Alice Springs
Bondi Beach
bush
corks
crocodiles
down under
G'day
koala
upside down

Europe
France

ambience
Arc de Triomphe
baguette
bistros
bonné chancé
boutiques
c'ést magnifiqué
Champs Elyseé
Channel tunnel
coffee or wine
Eiffel Tower
Elyseé
franc - ly
gay Pareé
in - seine
mérci
Notre Dame
par excellence
pavement cafes
plastered in Paris
romance
Seine
springtime in Paris
South Bank
to be franc
tout de suite
tunnel of love

Europe
Germany

Bavarian
Oktoberfest
best in my stein
bratwurst
fairytale castles
food
full marks
lager
mark my word
Oompah music
pleasure's all mein
Rhine
steins of bier
strudel
vineyards
wines
wunderbar

Europe
Italy

canna - letto myself
feel the pinch
Florence
Genoa better
gondola
it cannelloni be a
leaning tower
Naples
pasta my expectations
pastaport to Pisa
Pompeii
romance
Rome around
signorina
Venice
wine
worth every lira

North America
Canada

always get their man
buffalo
CN tower
crystal streams
dominion
falls down famously
fishing
go to great heights
goes down famously
Klondyke gold
lakes
lumber jack
mounties
Niagara Falls
plains
province
Rockies
spectacular scenery

North America
USA

at Liberty to
balance the bucks
baseball teams
Baywatch beauties
bet your bottom
Big Apple
bite of the Big Apple
Broadway
casinos
cheer leaders
dime
dimes make cents
dollar
burger bar
casino
Disneyland
gambling
Golden Gate
hamburgers
have a nice day
Las Vegas
liberates
makes cents
Manhattan
New York
out west
President
puts US in a
skyscrapers
spans the
star quality
stars and stripes
sunny weather
swim Atlantic for
Times Square
to the core of
United States
unites the states
way out west
White House
yanked out
yellow cabs

CHAPTER THREE
Words of Phrase

Constructing Phrases

Many compers find the step from brainstorming to penning an actual tiebreaker, too great. The secret is to build it up piece by piece.

There are several different ways and various styles you can adopt when writing tiebreakers, as you will see in the forthcoming chapters. To keep this exercise simple, let's assume we are going to write a two-line rhyming couplet using play on words. Entrants are asked to complete a tiebreaker in a lager competition, offering a prize trip to see a basketball game in America. The entry forms are available in off-licences and supermarkets, so no particular store is named. The product is clearly lager, whilst the prize and theme is American basketball games and in this example, we can forget the store. Make a list using words from either a brainstorming session under the two headings of product and theme, or words and phrases from our wordbank, such as these:

Product	Theme
lager	American basketball
taste	score
flavour	defends
number one brew	win - lose - nil
superior brew	leaders, cheer leaders
consistent quality	team
four packs	dream team
attack thirst	first class
no match	attack
ahead of the opposition	match
never overcharged	tradition
value	scores

Now we need to pull some of these words together to make phrases in preparation for writing the tiebreaker. It becomes an easy task to glance through your lists for words which have double meaning and can be used in word play, for example: 'thirst' choice. Your list may then appear as:

This dream team always scores
For quality and value they score the best
Store's shoppers know the score
Store's value is my 'thirst' choice
Defending quality when under attack
They cheer the winning team

Having decided we are going to use rhyme, you may like to use a rhyming dictionary. Let's see if there are any suitable words in the list.

score - more - adore - roar
attack - pack - back - lack

Now, should you be a beginner, don't think writing tiebreakers has to follow a rigid rule of words, then phrases, followed by the tiebreaker and the final perfecting or polishing of your entry. I have broken down the actual writing of the tiebreaker into four steps to help you. There are no hard and fast rules. This is a method I developed and is successful for me.

In some instances, as you make your phrases, and think of a rhyming word, for example: attack, the tiebreaker almost writes itself, as in:

They lead the pack defending quality when under attack

You will find as experience grows, more and more ideas come into play and you will have plenty of material to provide inspiration. Writing tiebreakers isn't easy. I've discovered you can't force inspiration. Sometimes I've spent hours playing around with words and ideas for a specific competition and getting nowhere at all, and have now learned to leave it alone and move onto something else. At other times, I've looked through a word list, had a sudden brainwave - yes, it happens sometimes - and my tiebreaker has been written in under ten minutes.

Race Against the Clock

One of the quickest competitions I entered and won, was in a travellers cheque contest in our local paper.

Having returned from holiday, I was late reading the newspaper, and noted the closing date for the contest was that day. However, most unusually, it gave a closing time of twelve noon. The newspaper office is only a five minutes drive away, and a glance at my watch revealed half an hour to the deadline. I quickly opened my *Intaslogans* wordbank at the appropriate pages. Ten minutes later, I drove round and deposited it safely in the box. Imagine my delight, when I subsequently received a phone call to say I had won first prize, £100 of travellers cheques.

I can also tell you anecdotes of hours spent searching for qualifiers, yet more hours writing and perfecting tiebreakers, only to post them off, never to be heard of again. But that's comping for you. The best advice I can give is keep an optimistic and positive approach. Be confident you can win and enjoy the challenge and fun this wonderful hobby has to offer. As soon as you've posted one competition, forget it and move on to the next. Then when you do win, it comes as a wonderful sur-prize.

A very good comping friend of mine, when interviewed on television, said, 'You'd be amazed at the prizes I've won, but if I told you how many I've entered and lost, you'd wonder why I bothered.' That sums it up nicely.

CHAPTER FOUR
On the Write Lines

Completing Tiebreakers

By this stage, you should have a much clearer idea of the way your tiebreaker is beginning to shape up. Your phrases may be simple `praise-the-products' or perhaps they have suitable endings which just lend themselves to rhyme. So how should the finished tiebreaker appear?

A look through several hundred tiebreakers from winners lists, revealed approximately 5% were written as one-line phrases, as in the old chestnut example:

    It makes life richer for the pourer

A chestnut, in case you're wondering, is a good winning tiebreaker which has been used time and again, and which keeps appearing on winners lists.

The majority of tiebreakers are written in rhyme with their word length being dependent on the word limit specified in competition rules. Popular limits tend to be no more than ten, twelve or fifteen words. However, there is nothing to stop entrants writing their tiebreaker in less than the word limit, unless you see the instructions 'write your tiebreaker in ten words', in which case you should strictly adhere to this.

Scansion

However you decide to construct your tiebreakers, they should all have one common factor - scansion. A completed tiebreaker should trip off the tongue and scan correctly. Try leaving them for a few hours or even days, returning with fresh eyes. Read them out loud, if you're still happy with them, post them off, otherwise, start again. Let's compare these two:

    No better selection would ever enhance our singles and CD selection
    No better selection to enhance a collection

Which do you prefer? The following tiebreakers all scan correctly:

    For just over a pound they make a beautiful sound
    Mixed or neat, it's hard to beat
    With a taste that's fresh, it out sparkles the rest

During one of my *Simply Slogans* weekend courses, we held a judging session, using recent winning tiebreakers. Coincidentally, amongst these was one which had been written by a lady in our group, although at the time, she didn't reveal which one it was.

When it came to the judging of the final few tiebreakers, I read out each one in turn. She remarked that I hadn't read hers out correctly. The emphasis, she told me, should have been placed on a specific word and not on the one I had used, thereby making it sound entirely different. It was a useful lesson for us all.

We cannot be there when the judging of our comps takes place, therefore, it is imperative tiebreakers should read and scan correctly. Should you need to emphasis a specific syllable or word, then this should be made clear by using inverted commas. When you bear in mind judges may spend only a few seconds on the initial reading of tiebreakers, there is no time for them to wonder where the writer wanted his or her emphasis placed.

There can be a tendency, having written tiebreakers for any length of time, to stick to the same old methods and style. All compers go through phases of lean spells, when the postman stops calling, except to deliver household bills. The reason may be the judges simply prefer other tiebreakers to yours, and you are doing nothing wrong at all. Your tiebreakers are apt, original, follow the lead-in line, scan correctly and even have a few eye-catching and choice words. Yet, there is a tendency to say 'what am I doing wrong, I can't even win a tee-shirt'.

In order to keep an optimistic approach to tiebreaker writing, sometimes it is advantageous to try out different ways of writing. Vary the styles you use, for example: alliteration, inversion or contrast. Look at the word length and scansion and use non-rhyme and rhyming compilations.

A useful tip, provided you are allowed multiple entries, is to submit several tiebreakers using different styles. Of course, the length of your tiebreakers will depend on the word limit allowed, but even here you can make changes. For example, should you be allowed twelve words, you may find you always use a two-line rhyming couplet with six words per line, as in:

> When days are boring and grey
> This product will whisk you away

You could try using the same number of words per line, but making your tiebreakers different by using punchier or selling-point words, punctuated by commas, for example:

> Consistent quality is what I seek
> Can after can, week after week

Alternatively, write the first line using five words, with seven on the second line, for example:

> Every surface has a lustre
> With just a single spray and duster

Non-rhyming One-liners

> A bear necessity for my creature comforts !
> It's the spread that takes the biscuit
> It can turn a 'kitchen sink drama' into an exciting 'who dunnit' !

Chapter Four : On the Write Lines 25

Rhyming Tiebreakers

Imagine you are asked to write a tiebreaker in six words, you may produce something along the lines of:

> Its excellent taste
> Guarantees no waste

Still using six words, you could change the way these are presented by choosing words which are punctuated by commas or exclamation marks. These could be words itemising information, selling points of the product or keywords, as in:

> Breakfast! lunch! dinner!
> Always a winner

When you are allowed to use seven words, you may use one line of four words, and one line of three, or vice versa, as in:

> Budget tight, price right   Awaken the napping
> Shine bright, dynamite   With alarm clock zapping

The more words you have to play with, the more ways you can write them, as in these eight, nine, ten, eleven, twelve and fifteen-word tiebreakers:

Eight words
It tastes so cheesy   Wide choice, helpful advice
And spreads so easy   Quality products, sensible price

Nine words
A night in style   Easily spreadable, deliciously edible
Would make my husband smile   So versatile with taste incredible

Dressed to stun
Ready for fun
Have I won ?   Yes, of course !

Ten words
Creamy cheese is just right   Taste healthy (product) dinners
When you want a megabyte   Turn choosy kids into cheese grinners

Eleven words
Passing every tastebud test   Character and taste equally shared
The King of beers beats the rest   Make (store) and (product) perfectly paired

Twelve words
Many hours of contented fun   Superior brew, refreshingly strong
Means peace and quiet for busy mum ! At (store)'s price, you can't go wrong

> Fifteen words
> (Product) stain, there's nothing so good
> For keeping the weather out of the wood
>
> Cool wine, sweet fruit, a tropical mix
> (Product) is my luxury for desert island disc

You will notice the majority of tiebreakers are written using rhyme. You can, however, make slight variations by using internal rhyme, as in:

> It's a sweet, that's a treat, anytime !

Two things to note here: firstly, words such as "it's" and "that's", should be counted as two words. Secondly, when competition rules state 'write a tiebreaker in less than ten words', it means just that. You may think I'm stating the obvious. Of course you know that less than ten words means no more than nine. You may be surprised to learn that up to 25% of all entries are disqualified for some infringement of rules, be it incorrect answers to the first part of the competition, exceeding word limits, omission of name and address (don't laugh, it does happen) or just plain unreadable entries !

Rhyme Time

Some compers find it easier to look through their list of brainstorming words to find one which will rhyme easily with others, for example: perfection. This rhymes with, affection, collection, complexion, detection, objection, protection, reflection, rejection and selection.

> I always get perfection from the finest (product) selection
> Superior flavour, brewed to perfection, friendly service, quality selection
> This superb selection enhances my complexion
> After using this selection, the others face rejection
> No finer selection for a pleasing reflection

You may have chosen the word 'reflection' for use in an entry. Using this at the end of a phrase, gives you a choice of words which will rhyme. Chances are several other compers will be thinking on the same lines, so you may decide to reposition it, as in:

> On reflection, these partners in shine give sparkling service, time after time
> Reflections speak louder than words

I am sure by taking a look at how you construct your tiebreakers within the word limits, will not only help you change your style, should you be 'stuck in a rut', but provide you with inspiration and encouragement to try different methods.

There are also many different styles of slogans too, which can be used to good effect. Write eye-catching tiebreakers using alliteration, contrast, inversion, adapting phrases, or any of the styles, examples of which you will find in chapters seven and eight.

CHAPTER FIVE
Intaslogans Winning Ways

Perfecting Tiebreakers

We have looked at how to construct tiebreakers, working through the three steps of brainstorming words, constructing phrases, and writing the tiebreaker.

Many compers then read through their finished tiebreaker and after checking they have completed all the tasks, and enclosed their qualifier, post it in good time for the closing date. They are then ready to start work on the next entry. Other compers, will leave the finished tiebreaker a few hours or even days and return to it with fresh eyes. Sometimes they find they can't improve it, so post it off. If they feel it can be improved, they then move onto step four, perfecting the tiebreaker.

This final stage can make all the difference between no prize and a runners-up prize or from runners-up prize to major prize. Just imagine for a moment, you've just heard the postman at the door. You collect the mail and amongst the bills suddenly spot a long white envelope, or LWE as compers like to refer to it. You tear open the envelope and, heart pounding, read those exciting words 'Congratulations, you have won a fantastic holiday in the Caribbean!' Okay, so have I convinced you ? Let's see how *Intaslogans* can help polish a tiebreaker:

Let's imagine you've written your tiebreaker for ground coffee, for which the prize is a day out at the races:

> Lynne's coffee always stays fresh for longer

You look through *Intaslogans : Drinks*, coffee section and can't find any words which give you further inspiration. You would like to introduce the horse racing theme, but no words spring to mind. You then turn to *Intaslogans : Sport,* horse racing and note:

ahead of the field	furlong
champion	leads the field
course	national winner
distance	steeplechasers
first past the post	strong finish
firm favourites	well-backed

You note `strong finish' and realise the word 'strong' has a double meaning, equally apt for coffee and a strong finish in horse racing. Playing around with the words may produce:

> Lynne's coffee always stays fresh for longer
> These favourites finish stronger

Then you notice the word 'furlong, which when extended to 'furlonger', sounds similar to 'for longer'. Thus your tiebreaker becomes:

> Lynne's coffee always stays fresh 'furlonger'
> These favourites finish stronger

Reading through this, you realise the scansion isn't right. The last line needs lengthening. So you ask yourself questions: what sort of favourites? Reading through the list of horse racing words you note:

> firm favourites
> well-backed

So now you have:

> Lynne's coffee always stays fresh `furlonger'
> These firm favourites finish stronger

Alternatively, you could say:

> Lynne's coffee always stays fresh 'furlonger'
> These well-backed favourites finish stronger

You may prefer the latter example, but feel 'well-packed' favourites would be a better choice, as this fits in with the coffee packaging. So, let's compare this with the original example:

> Lynne's coffee always stays fresh for longer

Which, when perfected, becomes:

> Lynne's coffee always stays fresh 'furlonger'
> These well-packed favourites finish stronger

I'm sure you'll agree the final tiebreaker is much better. In fact, this little gem won its author a major prize, and served as a useful example to illustrate the advantages of using wordbanks. Many compers think tiebreakers can be written in minutes, and often don't realise the amount of thought and hard work which goes into producing a brilliant tiebreaker. All too often we look through winners lists and think 'oh no, not another chestnut', then along comes a masterpiece of word play which we feel is a deserving winner.

Comping shouldn't be too serious. It's a fun, challenging and stimulating hobby. Assume an optimistic attitude. After all, if you say 'I won't win', then you probably won't. Tiebreaker completed, post it off and forget it. Until the long white envelope with:

> 'Congratulations, you have won ...' pops through your letter box.

Who says comping isn't exciting !

CHAPTER SIX
Personally Speaking

Having worked through our four steps of tiebreaker writing, let's now take a look at the lighter side of comping, before moving on to the next chapters, for more inspiration.

Comping is a wonderful hobby, not only does it challenge the mind with a variety of brain teasing tasks, but can transport you to exotic places halfway round the world. There's no greater thrill than opening a long white envelope, or LWE, as it is known by compers and reading the words 'Congratulations...' It doesn't really matter whether its a tee-shirt or a brand new car, it's the thrill of winning, having completed the task and been judged to have written the best tiebreaker from thousands of entries.

Comping can also be an isolated hobby. Now my husband has always completed crosswords and will help with anagrams and answering factual questions, but has no interest in writing tiebreakers whatsoever. After spending time looking round stores for entry forms, purchasing goods for your till receipt qualifiers, completing tasks, writing the tiebreaker, and sending it on its way, it's easy to become disillusioned, when the postman only brings you bills.

If you are a new comper, you will perhaps have to put up with the sniggers, giggles and comments of 'why do you bother - no-one ever wins!' Sound familiar? Well, when you win your first holiday or car, all that will change - as those of you who have done just that, will testify. The majority of compers go through bleak spells, sometimes for months on end, with not a single win in sight.

To renew enthusiasm, I like to look through my congratulatory letters and keep a positive and optimistic outlook. The tiebreakers you are writing today may well be tomorrow's winners. It helps to adopt a positive attitude and enjoy your hobby.

In those early comping days, six years ago, I didn't know anyone else who was at least remotely interested in competitions. It was only after reading Winn Sommor's competition page in our local newspaper the *Target*, did I begin to realise just how many 'compers' there were. She mentioned entry form services and competition magazines, all of which I'd never heard of. This was hardly surprising, considering they were not available in the newsagents, but only through subscription and mail order.

Winn with Lynne

I wrote to Winn, offering to swap entry forms and eventually we met and became good friends. I have her to thank for encouraging me to send in my first article to Kathy Kantypowicz, who was then Editor of *Winners Circle*, later renamed *Everyone's A Winner*. Not only were my first two articles accepted but I was invited to write a regular monthly column, which I did for two years until the magazine's demise. Kathy now edits *Competitors World*, and I have been privileged to become a regular contributor. Since then, I have met many compers and no longer feel this is an isolated hobby. Indeed the camaraderie is second to none and I've made some really wonderful friends - all thanks to comping.

After teaching my first 'How To Win Competitions' class at our local adult education centre, several of the 'students' didn't want the classes to end and asked if we could carry on meeting afterwards. So the Skegness Competitors monthly club was born. This was so successful, and we have long since ceased to be 'tutor' and 'students', to become good friends. Even as I write we are still going strong, sharing friendship, advice and offering encouragement. We have only one rule: each person brings a bottle of wine every time they have a win over £100. Believe me, we've shared some wine - even if they won't 'share' their till receipts !

The most marvellous thing about entering competitions for me, as well as the friendship, challenge and visiting exotic places, is that it has opened up a whole new world, including realising an ambition to become a journalist, and subsequently an author and magazine editor.

American Pie for Big Breakfast !

In 1992 I commenced writing my first comping book '*Win With Lynne - How To Win Consumer Competitions*', which was published and launched in October 1993. I sent a press release to a regional newspaper and was subsequently approached by a journalist from a national daily, who was interested in writing a story. The day the feature appeared, I answered the phone to a reporter from `Calendar News', asking if a crew could come round and film me. Having agreed to a time after lunch, I hastily dashed off to buy the newspaper and opened it to find a half page spread, complete with a photograph of me and my prize car !

Back home, I answered the phone to a DJ's Secretary, who asked if I would chat to them on their lunchtime radio programme next day. Having agreed, I decided I'd better have a quick tidy up before the `Calendar News' team arrived and then wondered why I'd bothered. They duly 'descended', set up lights and cameras around the house and began filming. Talk about exciting, I'd never appeared on TV before and this was as good as winning a prize itself !

In the midst of all the 'comings and goings', I answered the phone to a man who asked if I'd be willing to come down to London to appear next morning on `Big Breakfast'. I excitedly agreed and it was arranged my husband Trevor and I would catch the 6 pm train.

The `Calendar News' team left about four o'clock, so we hastily grabbed a bite to eat and started to pack some clothes and as many little prizes as we could cram into an overnight bag. Just as we were getting ready to leave, the phone rang again. I was rather disappointed to be told the `Big Breakfast' interview had been cancelled, so we unpacked the bag, made a cup of tea and plonked ourselves down on the settee - the first sit down we'd had all day - to watch `Calendar News'. Then decided we'd earned a night out.

Chapter Six : Personally Speaking

Whilst out, I took a phone call from my son, who said the Producer of 'Big Breakfast' had been on the phone and would I ring back. He asked if we'd come down and appear on the show. I replied, 'What, now?' So at eleven o'clock at night, instead of going to bed after what had been a rather hectic day, we hastily repacked the bag and drove to London.

We must have looked like zombies with no sleep, but were ushered into the studio canteen, and after several mugs of steaming hot coffee, felt a lot better. After that, there wasn't time to feel tired, as more people, camera crews, guests and presenters kept coming in and out.

The studio is set in a large house, and although the programme is very fast moving and appears chaotic, it is all down to split second timing.

Expecting a rehearsal, I was called through about 7.30 am and invited to sit on a settee with Gaby Roslin. I asked if we were having a run through, and was told 'No, we're on in... five seconds.'

Sitting behind a pile of my prizes, I was aghast to notice a pair of my white panties sitting on top of the portable TV set we'd brought with us. I hastily grabbed them and moved them out of sight. Suddenly we were on air, and Gaby was asking me about my prizes. She remarked 'I see you've even won some knickers,' to which I replied 'Oh yes', and tossed them nonchalantly into the air !

All too soon, it was over, and I headed back to the canteen to join Trevor for a slap up breakfast. No wonder they call it the 'Big Breakfast'. There were cereals, juices, fresh fruit, hot rolls, Danish pastries, Eccles cakes, steaming hot coffee, three types of eggs, bacon, sausages, hash browns, mushrooms, tomatoes and beans. You name it - it was there. Afterwards, we were given a tour of the studio, before being whisked away in a taxi back to our car.

My memorable faux pas of the day was when all the guests were asked to gather around a man singing and playing guitar, as the credits and music rolled for the final minutes. Singing away to 'American Pie', I said to the girl standing next to me, 'hey, isn't that Don McLean's song?' 'Yes', she said 'and THAT's Don McLean.' Oops !

Mid morning, still with no sleep, it was finally catching up with us, and we took turns to drive home. Suddenly, I remembered agreeing to appear on radio, so stopping on-route, I phoned through and explained where I was. So there I was, chatting away live on radio in the reception of a well-known roadside restaurant, much to the amusement of diners coming in and out.

We arrived home and went straight to bed, after being 'told-off' by my son who was most disappointed we hadn't brought him Craig Charles's autograph !

As my head hit a most welcoming pillow and sleep descended, I thought what a fantastic and memorable twenty-four hours it had been. But another one was to come later !

Game for a Show

After all the excitement had died down and life had returned to normal, I received a phone call from a lady in the Kelly Office at Ulster Television in Belfast. She had seen a feature about my book and prize wins in a national newspaper. As the Producer was putting together a programme on winners, they asked to see a copy of my book. Two weeks later, she rang and asked if I could come over to Belfast the following Friday evening.

Trevor and I were sent flight tickets and at 6 pm we soared into the air, leaving behind a foggy Leeds airport. Already feeling like VIP's, sipping wine and eating a delicious evening meal, it felt as if we'd only been airborne for minutes rather than an hour. Soon we were descending into Belfast City airport. We were just wondering where to wait, when we were paged and ushered outside by a chauffeur into a waiting limousine. Oh, is this what it feels like to be a film star, I wondered.

We were taken to a luxurious hotel, where another delicious evening meal awaited us. However, we could only manage the coffee. Must be the only time I've refused sherry trifle and cream-laden chocolate gateaux !

The chauffeur explained the `Kelly Show' didn't commence until 11 pm and he would come back for us about 10 pm. Relaxing in the lounge, sipping cocktails and listening to the grand piano, we tried to guess, without success, who was who.

Before long it was time to go to the Ulster Television Centre, where we were greeted warmly by Helena, who had made all our arrangements. In the upstairs bar, overlooking the studio, I was introduced to Maureen who had won countless game shows, Mike who'd just published his book on lottery winners and another Mike who'd just won £1.8 million on the Irish lottery.

Down in make-up, I casually asked one man who he was, and he introduced himself as the actor who played Jimmy Corkhill on Brookside. Never having seen the programme, of course I'd not recognised him, nor his co-star character, Anna. However, I did recognise the Barron Knights.

Back in the bar, taking care only to drink orange juice, I watched fascinated as the studio audience began to fill up, lights came on, and a warm up artiste went through his paces, to put them at their ease. What about us? I thought - nerves starting to creep in. 'Do we get a rehearsal?' I tentatively enquired of Helena. 'No, but you'll be fine,' she replied warmly. And she was right.

Before long, Maureen and I were ushered downstairs and during the commercial break, led to the sofa to sit by the presenter, Gerry Kelly. He greeted us warmly, and with the make-up artiste brushing powder over the end of our noses, the seconds countdown started, cameras whirred, and we were on.

Chapter Six : Personally Speaking   33
___

I suddenly thought, 'Wow, this is fantastic!' The nerves disappeared and leaning back on the settee, I relaxed, chatted about comps and thoroughly enjoyed every minute of it. In fact, I was rather disappointed when it was all over and we were shown out of the studio and back into the bar. This time, I did have a martini - I felt I'd earned it.

After the show, all the guests chatted like long lost friends, and the snacks, nibbles and hot sausage rolls soon disappeared. The Assistant Producer suggested we all go back to the hotel to continue the party. The memory of singing songs outside the studio with Pete of the Barron Knights, whilst waiting for the limousine, will stay with me for the rest of my life.

Back at the hotel, there was no longer any need to 'guess who was who', as we listened to how Mike had won his million pounds and then told his wife off for 'extravagantly spending £200' in one afternoon. Life on the road as a long running and famous band wasn't as glamorous as it sounds, we found out, listening to tales from the Barron Knights. 'Never mind jet lag,' said Pete, 'we often suffer hotel lag.' 'What's that?' I enquired, 'when you come out of the bedroom in the middle of the night to go to the bathroom, to find it's not where it was last night, 'cos you're in a different hotel,' he chuckled.

At 5.30 am we crawled into bed, and it seemed only five minutes before the alarm was ringing out its 7 am call. We ate a delicious breakfast amid more friendly banter. All too soon, it was time to say our goodbyes and be whisked, once again in the limousine, to the airport. Goodness, was it really less than twelve hours since we'd arrived there !

Intacomps

Following the 'Gerry Kelly Show' appearance, I received many orders for my book from both Northern Ireland and Eire. However, I was surprised to be given a letter by my postman Brian one morning, all the way from Malaysia. Now who did I know there? No-one. Had I won a holiday? Upon opening it, I was stunned to find an order for my book. Now where had this come from? It certainly was a mystery. Since then, further orders were received from France, the Sultanate of Oman and Hong Kong. So maybe it is a small world, after all !

Around this time, I decided to fulfil my ambition to edit a competition magazine, and June 1994, saw the birth of *Intacomps*. Produced quarterly, this newsletter lists details of current competitions including free-to-enter and magazine competitions, news, views, comping trivia, features, reference section, an on-going compers course, letters page and tiebreakers for inspiration.

Of course, one of the first copies was sent to my friend Winn Sommor, who not only produces an annual competition booklet herself, but writes for the Lincolnshire *Target* newspaper. Winn then sent me the following feature for *Intacomps*:

Letter to the Editor by Winn Sommor
September 1994 - Intacomps

Well Lynne, you've finally gone and done it ! I wonder if you remember what you said your ambition was, in one of your letters to me, after we'd been corresponding for about three months. Yes, that's right - to edit a comping magazine.

I had just commenced writing my comping articles *The Competitors' World* for the Lincolnshire based *Target* newspaper. I had invited readers to write to me and you were one of the first to do so. You suggested we swap entry forms, which I agreed. We began corresponding regularly and as our friendship grew, you revealed your comping ambition to me.

At that time, of course, although you had won a few very nice small prizes, none of these had been with tiebreakers and you had yet to win a major prize. Plus the fact you had never written a comping article, let along had one published !

I suppose you thought me rather rude and blunt when I said in my reply that 'NO-ONE is going to buy a magazine written by a complete unknown. People like to read an introduction something as follows: Mrs X has won countless prizes, including a car, holidays and cash as well as numerous runners-up prizes and is well known in the competitors world for her articles featured in...'

I suggested you try and get some articles published in well known comping magazines and win a few more substantial prizes. I advised you of one or two magazines to submit articles to and within a short time your first was accepted. Not only that, you then won a holiday, followed by a car, both won with tiebreakers.

Later of course, you wrote your first book, *Win With Lynne - How To Win Consumer Competitions*. I say 'first' because knowing you I don't think you'll stop at one. It certainly came as no surprise to me to learn you were going to launch *Intacomps* - it seemed the logical next step. Well, what can I say now ! If the first issue of *Intacomps* is just a taste of what is to come, then I know it is going to be extremely successful.

My 50th *The Competitors' World* article appeared in the *Target* last month and without the feedback from the readers it wouldn't have been possible to write so many. I do hope your readers will write to you with interesting comping trivia and stories of their own successes, failures and amusing experiences. Readers contributions are so very important.

My New Year's Resolution was to 'Win a biggie' and my ambition is to win a family holiday. Will you please write back Lynne and advise me what I should do to achieve this - feel free to be as rude and as blunt as possible as, I've learned from experience, it just might do the trick!

Congratulations on an excellent first issue of *Intacomps*. You don't happen to want an Assistant Editor by any chance do you ?

Winn Sommor

Chapter Six : Personally Speaking

Weekends of Course !

In October 1993, the same month as the book's launch, I held a *Win With Lynne - How to Win Consumer Competitions* weekend in a hotel in Skegness. This was a first for Lincolnshire, and saw compers travelling from parts of Lincolnshire, Yorkshire and as far as Southampton to attend. Aimed at beginners or those with some experience of competitions, it covered information on where to find entry forms, the types of competition tasks and how to enter including writing tiebreakers and of course, social evenings and competitions.

Some compers expressed a wish to return the following year but quite naturally, didn't want to cover the same programme. So I introduced an 'advanced' weekend entitled *Simply Slogans*, which was organised in November 1994 at a seafront hotel in Skegness. News spread and more compers attended, travelling from many parts of the country and as far afield as Jersey in the Channel Islands.

Simply Slogans

The *Simply Slogans* weekend, as its name implies, covered many aspects of slogan writing. This included tips and hints on how to write winning tiebreakers, whilst looking at the many different styles and adding sparkle to slogans. Compers had an opportunity to become involved in a mock judging session, which proved very beneficial, as they were able to 'view tiebreakers from the other side of the fence.'

An optional treasure hunt was organised for the Saturday afternoon, which proved quite popular, plus social evenings and competitions. There was also much laughter, including an amusing anecdote related by one of our guests.

Apparently, she and her new found friend, were following the treasure trail, when they stopped in their tracks, having spotted the magic word WIN. Disappearing into the busy store, they noted the competition task was to watch the demonstration video tape of 3-D moving 'magic-eye' pictures and guess what they were. The television and video was situated just in front of the counter, and she bent down to take a closer look. She was unable to guess the object, so rewound the video and tried again. Still puzzled, she then lay down on the floor to get a closer look, rewinding the video once again.

The shop was quite crowded being a typical Saturday afternoon, and customers had to either move around or step over her to reach the counter. Eventually, the long suffering and patient Manager, must have decided enough was enough. He casually strolled over to her friend, tapped her on the shoulder and said 'Madam, please tell your friend it's a dinosaur!'

A dinosaur !
Are you sure ?

Compers are able to return each autumn, year after year, to renew enthusiasm, learn additional skills and make new friends. Part of the November 1995 *Simply Slogans* weekend was filmed by Granada Television, which was shown on 'This Morning' in February 1996.

Intacomps Days

A few months after *Intacomps* had been launched, and several lovely readers letters had been received, I thought it would be a great idea to hold one-day social events for compers, whether beginners, experienced or just in-between. After all, not all compers want to attend a course, but do like to meet other like-minded people, swap entry forms and enjoy social get-togethers. With this in mind, the first *Intacomps* day was held in December 1994 in Skegness.

A few days before it was due to run, I received a phone call out of the blue from a production company, who wanted to know when my next event was to be held, as they'd like to film it. I was certainly agreeable but didn't know how the compers attending would feel about it, so a few hectic hours followed whilst I tried to contact them all. The news was greeted by a mixture of excitement including one lady who said, 'Glad you told me, it will give me time to get a new dress and my hair done.' Winn Sommor was my first guest speaker on the day, and I'll let her take up the story, by printing her article which was featured in the Lincolnshire *Target*.

oooooOOOooooo

The Competitor's World by Winn Sommor
December 1994 - Target, Lincolnshire newspaper

I'm sure you will recall I told you I would be going along to a 'Comping Day' in Skegness on Saturday 3 December. What an exciting day it turned out to be!

What I and other keen compers did not know when we originally decided to attend was that the compers were not going to be the only people to invade the hotel for the day. We were joined by a five strong film crew researching and recording for the BBC 'Good Morning' programme which will include a series of eight short comping related features.

Lynne Suzanne had no idea there would be extra guests attending until the Wednesday before the event when she received a telephone call completely out of the blue from a representative from the BBC who wanted to know when she would be holding her next comping event. When she told them she had a day event planned for Saturday, she was staggered when they told her they would like to come and film the whole proceedings.

Although Lynne had no objections herself she immediately made every effort to contact everyone who was attending the comping day, not only to 'warn' them but to make sure that no-one had any strong objections to their presence.

Lynne has got used to being in front of the cameras by now and has even appeared on Ulster Television on the 'Gerry Kelly Show' for which she was flown out to Belfast and stayed at a plush hotel, earlier this year. Lynne is well aware, however, that the very thought of television cameras can be a daunting experience to some people so she wanted to be absolutely sure no-one would feel intimidated by it all.

Chapter Six : Personally Speaking

I travelled over to Skegness on the Friday evening as Lynne had invited me to stay the night at her home. Although we had kept in touch by telephone and letter we had not actually seen each other since we both attended the weekend 'Comp Camp' in Scarborough two years ago, so as you can imagine we had lots to talk about.

Issue Three of Lynne's quarterly newsletter *Intacomps*, had just been despatched to subscribers and Lynne asked me to judge the caption competition which had appeared in Issue Two. She gave me a pile of sentences to look through . I think it must have been a case of 'great minds think alike' because the one I chose as a winner, was also Lynne's choice !

It was the first time I had been to Lynne's home and I was privileged to be shown into the smallest room in the house which Lynne had turned into her comping 'den'. On one long wall was an impressive array of neatly displayed posters, photographs, entry forms and congratulatory letters, all connected with her major prize wins. Towards one end of the wall, set slightly apart from the rest, were a couple of large posters and Lynne told me with a grin 'That's where I've been' and, turning slightly, pointed to the posters at the far end of the room and said 'and that's where I'm going.'

Those posters are Lynne's 'winspiration' and yes, I'm as confident as Lynne is that she will get there. Only that very week I had been one of the first she had confided in that she had just received notification of a first prize win of a two-week holiday in Margarita, a small island near Trinidad and Tobago.

After spending an evening with Lynne, I am now convinced I know the secret of her incredible success. It must be the endless cups of tea that she drinks which keeps her 'little grey cells' in perfect comping working order. In just four hours on the Friday evening, she managed to drink eight large cups of tea !

On the Saturday morning Lynne and I arrived at the hotel just before 9 am and the crew of a director, presenter, researcher, sound technician and cameraman arrived shortly afterwards. The 'comping' guests started to arrive about 9.30 am and over coffee Lynne and Gillian the Director, explained that the comping day would go ahead just as planned and we should aim to carry on as if the crew were not there.

This did prove to be rather difficult for some people having been split up into groups for a 'brainstorming' session, trying to come up with a minimum of three tiebreakers in about half an hour and a microphone hovering two feet above your head and cameras facing towards you just a couple of yards away !

Most of us did manage to settle down, however, and the tiebreakers we created in small groups were judged later by everyone present.

Another session later in the day was judging actual tiebreakers from a genuine winners list. These consisted of the first prize winners completion, ten runners-up plus four 'red herrings' thrown in for good measure, all mixed up in no particular order. Each little group took part in role play which we had to judge the tiebreakers from different angles. I, for instance, was a factory manager, one of the group of three representatives from a French cheese producer, others were representatives from the supermarket who promoted the competition, the handling house, personnel from the Paris travel company who were providing the prizes and independent judges. Although we had to assess each competition from these viewpoints we also had to consider each on its overall merit. Selections were made by everyone and the votes added up, which narrowed it down to just three for final consideration for the major prize. The little groups voted once more to come up with an overall winner.

It was interesting to note that the 'compers' choice was not the genuine one that actually won, it was only voted second by us. Although I had managed to 'guess' which was the genuine winner, my personal favourite was actually the one the 'compers' had voted third. Voting was very close and we all felt we had benefited by taking our role play seriously rather than just selecting the one we liked best from a purely personal viewpoint.

The Abbey Hotel had laid on a lovely three-course lunch for us and ample cups of tea and coffee during the much needed breaks. There were lots of different competitions to take part in during the day, group discussions and plenty of opportunities to chat and get to know other people.

Neil, who had travelled from Humberside, was the only male comper present but didn't seem too perturbed to be among ladies who had travelled from various areas in Norfolk and Lincolnshire. Amongst Neil's' impressive list of wins were two trips on Concorde !

Towards the end of the day prizes for the individual and group competitions were awarded. I had donated a voucher for a copy of my next booklet but most of the prizes were assorted boxed chocolates. We all waited with bated breath to see who was going to win the much coveted prize of a tee-shirt and baseball cap. This was won by a member of the Boston club. Lynne did try to coax her to give the prize back by bribing her with the offer of her prize holiday in exchange, but she simply wouldn't hear of it !

Although Lynne managed to keep to the original programme as much as possible, having the camera crew there did mean we became progressively more and more behind schedule as the day wore on. The activities should have ended about 4 pm but at 5 pm we were still going strong. Steve, the researcher, had also requested as many people as possible to stay behind later to take part in individual interviews. By the time I eventually returned to Boston it was almost 8 pm.

It had been a great day out, however, and if the compers had been requested to sum up the day in just one word among these I am sure would have been - fun - educational - informative - enlightening - exciting. But the one word I would have used would have been EXHAUSTING!

So, spare a thought for the film crew, particularly Dick the cameraman, who was rather slim and could have been no more than five feet six inches - moving that heavy camera around and positioning it at awkward angles must have been no mean feat.

I spoke to Lynne a couple of days later on the phone and she told me it was about 9.30 pm before the crew finally left the hotel.

Chapter Six : Personally Speaking 39

It certainly was interesting to see what goes on behind the scenes, a twelve hour working day, hours of filming and at the end of it careful editing to perhaps produce less than half an hours actual film.

Well I really must close now. Time to put the kettle on. I've only had five cups of tea today. Watch out, Lynne - I aim to win !

Winn Sommor

oooooOOOooooo

The second *Intacomps* day was arranged for the following April, and although some compers had returned, they were able to make new friends, as by this time, numbers had grown. So as the day lacked the air of excitement of the previous day, which was generated by the film crew, was the day just as enjoyable? Again, Winn takes up the story.

The Competitor's World by Winn Sommor
May 1995 - Target, Lincolnshire newspaper

I can describe the English weather in just one word 'unpredictable'. If you had seen Lynne Suzanne and myself battling against the cold, high winds and rain on 22 April, you would certainly understand why!

The weather was almost identical to 3 December 1994, and we were heading for the same venue, the Abbey Hotel on the seafront at Skegness to attend an *Intacomps* comping day. The only difference this time was that the holiday season had started which meant we had to park the car two streets away instead of on the roadside opposite the hotel.

The cold wind had made my eyes run and despite their claims, a certain hairspray did not keep my hair in place ! The only consolation Lynne and I had was that we arrived early and had the chance to repair the damage before the other guests arrived.

I am sure regular readers will recall the December 1994 first *Intacomps* comping day turned out to be quite an event as it was filmed for a slot in the 'How To Be A Winner' feature on the BBC 'Good Morning' programme shown earlier this year.

I really was not expecting the comping day to be so interesting or as entertaining but I was proved wrong ! Several of the Boston club members had also made a return visit and found, like me that it was just as enjoyable. As well as people from various areas in Lincolnshire guests had also travelled from Huntingdon, Nottinghamshire and Leicestershire was well represented by a mother and three of her daughters.

Before getting into the 'serious' activities we were served with tea and coffee and spent a little time breaking the ice. Anne from Lincoln was convinced we had met before so we went over several places where we had both worked and visited in an effort to conform but to no avail. So trying to be helpful, I said, 'Perhaps you have seen me on television' - referring to my few brief moments of fame on the 'How To Be A Winner' feature. 'Ah yes, that's it - I knew it,' Anne immediately responded with a twinkle in her eyes 'You are the lady who appeared in that film with Richard Gere !'

At this point we both burst out laughing and I knew I had met a soul mate, thinking to myself now here is lady with a whacky sense of humour, just like me.

This was confirmed later that morning when we just happened to be put into the same group for a 'brainstorming' tiebreaker session. Each group were required to come up with a minimum of three in a limited amount of time. Anne created a rather amusing tiebreaker. It would certainly have made any judges in the genuine judging session titter but wouldn't have won any prizes ! Just for a bit of a light-hearted fun, however, she decided to submit it anyway but instead of putting our group number four down on the paper as the originators she wrote group three instead. When all the tiebreakers were read out aloud later in the day, it certainly created a laugh, the only trouble was all Boston members eyes turned in my direction. 'It wasn't me' I protested, but I don't think they believed me.

Some people had travelled on their own and did not know a soul when they arrived. An outsider looking in on us at lunch time would have found it hard to believe that many of the people chatting away happily had been total strangers just three hours previously. Compers are certainly among the friendliest and most generous people I know and are happy to share their hints, knowledge and advice with those new to the hobby.

As well as group tiebreaker and judging sessions there were individual competitions to enter and plenty of breaks to socialise. One competition consisted of just one question: 'How long is a piece of string?' We were told there was quite a logical answer to this yet none of us came up with the 'correct' answer. When the many and varied answers were read out, all were certainly logical and some were brilliant - definitely far more ingenious than the 'right' version! Lynne Suzanne was so impressed with our brain power that the answers will be listed in a future issue of her *Intacomps* magazine.

All too soon the events were drawing to a close and if Lynne (who had put a lot of time and effort into organising the day) had any doubts about its success they were soon squashed. Someone had asked a member of the Leicester family if they had found it worthwhile coming all that distance just for a day. 'Well', she replied, 'none of us has said hoist today.' This met with puzzled looks all round. We were then privileged to be let into the secret of the family code word. Apparently whenever the family attend a function not quite knowing what to expect or if they are going to enjoy themselves and any of them feel uncomfortable with the situation, all they have to say to the others is 'hoist'. Then they all immediately get up and make a hasty departure !

The comping day was certainly great fun and I made some new pen friends in the process. I still keep in touch with Neil from Humberside who I met at the first social day last December. I seem to have the knack of winning outsize tee-shirts but Neil specialises in winning exciting holidays and recently wrote to tell me about his latest - an all expenses two week trip to Sri Lanka !

Chapter Six : Personally Speaking

'Am I disheartened?' Not a bit of it, as like all keen compers, I am convinced my big win is just around the corner.

Winn Sommor

oooooOOOooooo

Intacomps goes Nationwide

After the second day was held, news spread, and requests to hold events in other areas were made. The first day held outside Lincolnshire was in Sheffield in August 1995. This was well attended with compers coming from parts of surrounding districts and as far afield as Huddersfield, Manchester and Bath.

I had decided to ask compers if they would like to join in a one-day National Lottery syndicate as I had devised a system of bankers and permutations, similar to that used for our `order of merit' competitions. Twenty compers joined in and we had jokingly arranged to meet next morning, should we win the jackpot.

Tuning into the television that Saturday evening, I couldn't believe my eyes when the first of our banker numbers was drawn out. Excitement mounted when the second banker number was drawn, which was followed by two more of our numbers. Although we didn't win the jackpot, we did have nine winning lines out of the twenty we had placed. So just how close were we? Well, the next numbers to the two remaining ones we had chosen were drawn out. With just one more number, we would have shared £92,000. And both numbers, well, I would have been writing this in the Bahamas !!!

At the October 1995 Skegness event, the one-day lottery syndicate was held again. This time we went to the other extreme and didn't have one number drawn out of eighteen chosen. It was summed up nicely by Neil from Humberside, who wrote: `Thanks for a wonderful day. All I shall say about the lottery is we should have splashed out £2 each and permed all the other numbers that we didn't have in our first perm.` Nicely put.

One lady, who had attended the Sheffield event was a relative newcomer to comps. She had entered a few years ago with some success but after a long no-comping lapse, had returned to them. She needed to be aware of new and changing judging trends and wanted to meet other compers for inspiration. Fired with enthusiasm, she came over to Skegness in October for the next *Intacomps* day. Then a month later, she phoned me in a state of uncontrolled excitement and joy. She'd just scooped first prize in a national tiebreaker competition with a prize which had been her ambition, to travel on the Orient Express. 'What I feel swung it for me,' she said 'was the use of two descriptive and apt words, which I felt summed up the whole theme of the contest.' 'Will you be coming to the next day in Sheffield?' I asked her. 'Yes, definitely - unless I'm away on another prize holiday,' she added with a laugh.

Then in December, I received a letter from a lady who had travelled from Manchester to the Sheffield day. `Thank you for all the advice you gave on slogan writing', she said, `I've had two runners-up prizes of video tapes and now I've just won my first car, a Seat Ibiza. I nearly didn't send it off. I'm very glad that I did ! My next dream now, is a really exotic holiday'. I'm sure you'll have noticed the very positive `my *first* car'. I'm sure it will be too !

It's so lovely to hear of other's success. 'Why do you hold days and give winning advice?' was a question I was asked by a radio presenter, 'surely, you should keep the competition details to yourself so you can win.' All I could think of on the spur of the moment was to say there are literally hundreds of competitions each and every week and far more than you or I could possibly enter. In fact, enough for everyone to have a go at.

Let's face it, if we all keep entering, the promoters sales will increase and encouraged by an enthusiastic response, are likely to organise more competitions, which is an advantage for all of us. The other bonus I've found, is the friendship. I've met so many lovely people through comping and made so many new friends. Non-compers tend to think we are all arch enemies, but that's not the case at all. As I'm sure you've found out too.

Although the *Intacomps* programmes are similar, each day is unique. The tiebreakers used for analysis are all from recent winning lists. Advice is given on how competitions are judged and there is always an opportunity to ask questions.

You may even win a prize in a variety of comps from a trivia quiz, to anagrams, wordgames, factual question comps and even an optional individual tiebreaker comp. Even if you attended every event, you would still find plenty of compers to chat to. Some of whom may be familiar faces, perhaps new friends you made last time. Travelling from all parts of the UK, there will be complete beginners to comping, experienced compers and many just in-between. Whether you've come to learn, swap entry forms, enter the comps or just to have a pleasant day out and chat to new friends over lunch, we all have something in common - a love of competitions.

You can be sure the one-day lottery syndicate will feature as part of the comping programme at all future *Intacomps* days and *Simply Slogans* weekends, which will be held in hotels in various parts of the country. Should you be interested in attending, then please do drop me a line, to the address given on page 100, and I'll be pleased to send you details.

As I mentioned earlier, I have Winn to thank for setting me on the road to writing. Not only, have both Winn and I had several articles featured in competition magazines but we have both published booklets and you can read about Winn's unique annual competition publication in chapter ten.

From the acceptance of my first competition article, I now write regular columns for the press, and features have appeared in the *Grimsby Telegraph, South Wales Argus, Chester Chronicle, Evening Chronicle* - Newcastle Upon Tyne, *Belfast Telegraph* and the *Daily Mail*.

And now I've fulfilled my ambition to become a journalist, write a book and edit a comping magazine. `What now?' I'm sure Winn will ask.

Well, my ambition is to write my third comping book, which I'm already researching for, and to become a television presenter with my own comping programme.
I'll let you know what time it's on ! ***Lynne***

CHAPTER SEVEN
Styles of Slogans

Play on Words

Having covered the four steps I use for writing winning tiebreakers, let's now move on to take a look at a variety of styles which can be used, commencing with word play.

Assuming a competition allows multiple entries, you may wish to vary your tiebreakers, thereby enhancing your chances of success.

The only type of contest where I advise using the same tiebreaker is for order of merit tasks. This is because your chances of arriving at the same order as the judges, is a lot less than when giving answers to factual questions, which can be researched. Imagine then, having submitted six entries, and the one with the matching line which goes through for judging contains the worst of your six tiebreakers. Far better to use the same good tiebreaker on all entries.

Pink Carnations

Do pause and have a quick look through *Prizewinning Slogans* in chapter nine. I wonder how many different styles you can identify. You will almost certainly have noticed nearly every tiebreaker is written in rhyme. There is nothing wrong with this at all, but you may be onto a winner, should you submit a non-rhyming entry.

Consider for a moment, five judges sitting around a table, wading through list after list of tiebreakers, on a computer printout. They read through similar sounding tiebreakers and this must be quite tedious at times. How refreshing then, to come across something different.

On my *Simply Slogans* courses, I liken this to a room full of ladies all wearing plain dark coloured suits. A glance round the room reveals nothing different. Then in walks a lady, also in a dark coloured suit, but sporting a bright pink carnation on her lapel. How this stands out. All eyes turn towards her.

This then is the effect you should strive to achieve when writing your own entries. The pink carnation. This could be a non-rhyming slogan amidst a sea of rhyming entries. An interesting coined word. A play on words. Or how about a sparkle of humour?

Pictures Worth a Thousand Words

It is difficult to set a scene or paint a picture, when you've only got ten words to get the message across. Try bringing an already established scene into the minds of the judges.

If I say 'Cinderella', what picture does that conjure up for you? You may 'see' Cinders in her tatty rags, slaving over the kitchen stove. You may 'see' the look of wonder on her face, as her fairy godmother turns the pumpkin into a golden carriage. You may be more of a romantic and 'see' the handsome Prince place a glass slipper on the foot of a beautiful girl in a luxurious ball gown. All this and I've only used one word - Cinderella.

To illustrate this point further, in what I feel is a most worthy winning tiebreaker, let us 'picture' the following scene. Entrants were asked why they would love to win a brand new set of kitchen appliances supplied by a well-known store. The word limit was a generous, twenty-five words. Firstly, the sentence completion begins by praising the appliances:

> Dazzling appliances, so efficient

Four words and already we can 'see' these lovely kitchen appliances, and we are told they are efficient. The word sums it up nicely. No need to use a lot of unnecessary words as in:

> These kitchen appliances look very nice gleaming
> away in my work area and they work very well too

What a mouthful ! Dazzling appliances, so efficient. Says it all, doesn't it. By all means if you find it easier to say what you mean then do write it down, but then go back over it and chop out unnecessary words. Then it moves on to expand the picture:

> Dazzling appliances, so efficient, make Cinderella more proficient

Now we are not left in any doubt as to the role in which Cinders has been cast. Here she's not the glamorous belle of the ball, but the work weary Cinders in her tatty rags slaving away for the two ugly sisters. The eight word tiebreaker sentence works well as it stands, and in a contest which has a ten word limit, you could add a couple more words and a final polish and you're on the winning route. Given a twenty-five word limit, the author of this winning tiebreaker, then expanded the story by explaining just what poor old Cinders had to do:

> Washing, cleaning, cooking for gluttons

Gluttons. What a lovely word. I'm sure you'll agree 'gluttons' sums up the ugly sisters nicely. Then comes the finale. The pink carnation.

> All from pressing (product)'s 'Buttons'

Brilliant. The punch line comes right at the end - in this case, the play on words, which is so apt to the story of Cinderella. So let's look at the complete tiebreaker:

> Dazzling appliances, so efficient, make Cinderella more proficient,
> At washing, cleaning, cooking for gluttons, all from pressing (product)'s 'Buttons' !

The author of this brilliant little masterpiece is now the worthy owner of a kitchenful of dazzling, efficient appliances. A very deserving winner, I'm sure you'll agree.

Chapter Seven : Styles of Slogans

To bring a play on words into your entries you need to find some suitable words. Glancing through *Intaslogans* wordbank will spark off ideas and help you with your choice. You may like to highlight these using a yellow marker pen for future reference. Alternatively, make a separate list using a page for each product or theme. By adding to your list whenever a word or phrase catches your eye, you will have some relevant material for inspiration.

Homonyms and Homophones

A homonym is a word having the same pronunciation and spelling as another word but with a different meaning.

A homophone is a word having the same pronunciation as another word but with different spelling and meaning. Which reminds me, did you hear the story of the bride who, upon entering the church, noticed her husband-to-be and promptly declared: 'Aisle alter hymn'.

You can use homonyms and homophones to good effect in your tiebreakers. You may find the following examples useful to get you started:

Homonyms

Cut	Edit, shorten / a style / carve, chop / a gash 'Cut' for action, (clothing)'s 'star' and give 'premiere' satisfaction
Dish	Satellite dish / to give out / a bowl / a course Their systems are programmed to 'dish up' lowest prices
Kick	To boot, strike / abandon, break They know how to 'kick' your thirst (football theme)
Line	Washing line / football pools line / cable, cord / business / ancestry This home banker gives the best results to get a winning 'line' (soap powder)
Mull	To chew over / name of a place They only select the best and don't 'mull' over the rest
Net	A mesh, netting / earn, to gain / clear (Store) is the best place to 'net' the bargains (tennis theme)
Packet	Container, carton / slang term for money Delicious and nutritious, it won't cost 'a packet' at (store)
Pinch	To nip / chafe, hurt / pilfer / a speck, taste Shopping here is a cinch, I go Italian without feeling the pinch !

Present	A gift / here and now, available / to introduce
	These tokens point the way to a present in the future
Reception	Greeting / receiving / function, party
	Great 'reception', savings 'sky' high and (product) they supply
Sweet	Confectionery / syrupy / affectionate / aromatic, fresh / melodious
	Freedom has an orange shape, perfect for a 'sweet' escape (holiday prize)
Take	To accompany / accept / abduct /shooting film
	For a self catering break it's the ideal 'take' (holiday prize)
Tonic	A pick-me-up / a drink, e.g. gin and tonic
	'Spirits' low, finances chronic, (product) is the perfect 'tonic'
View	On show / to watch / an opinion
	Warm 'reception', bargains on 'view', choice extensive, pleasing price too

Homophones

A wash	
Awash	Powder and machine are both a'wash with efficiency
Brakes	
Breaks	(Product)'s glue is all it takes, when there's only seconds to fix the 'brakes'
Buy	
By	There's nothing (product)'s overlook, wherever I'm going, I go 'buy' the book
Board	
Bored	(Product) easily gets awards for brightening the 'cheese-bored'
Great	
Grate	For a snack or main meal, cheddar has 'grate' appeal
Hangar	
Hanger	It would fly my washing from take-off to 'hanger' without turbulence
Meat	
Meet	It's the perfect plate to 'meat' your mate (romance theme)
Mustard	Channel hopping would be magnifiqué, so I've 'mustard' up my hopes and I'm
Mustered	free next week!
Paws	
Pours	This human animal takes pride, in cleansing 'paws' and protecting the 'hide'

Chapter Seven : Styles of Slogans 47

Putt
Put   Great (product), super store, 'putt' together who needs more (golf holiday)

Reel
Real   They landed a 'reel' catch

Sane
Seine   For chores indoors , 'Seine' shoppers all make tracks for (store)

Tales
Tails   It contains 'tails' of the unexpected (safari holiday)

Thirst
First   With (product) you come alive, out of 'thirst' into four wheel drive (car prize)

Wheel
We'll   There is no miss-steak 'wheel' meat again (cycling theme)

These 'playful' tiebreakers have all won prizes for their authors:

'After hours' on the Seine, confidence will win whilst perspiration wanes
At this health farm there would be no spare types for this bicycle 'belle'
Feeling boxed in, I w(h)ine for the 'grape' escape
For once I will not mind being a near 'miss'
From the very first movement you know the 'score', (product) performs without a flaw
Guaranteed more for less, I'm gratefully 'flushed' with success
He 'nose' I'm 'scent-sational'
I am one hundred 'per scent' sure of exuding feminine allure
I know its 'odour whelming'
In the wise 'buy' election, it's the greatest soap selection
It's winning formula makes good 'scents', ensuring intimate moments without offence
It gives me the 'scent' of protection
It sprays 'misty' for me
(Product) at (store)'s prices won't make my basket 'bawl' !
(Product) produce world champions, (store) 'soccer' it to you
They 'dish' up heavenly quality at earthly prices
They 'spin' through your wash with speed, efficiency and brilliance
They make a 'thirst' class team, quality and value score supreme
With (product) achieve my dream, the 'cycle-ogical' advantage is supreme

When using play on words, there is no need to adhere rigidly to using homonyms and homophones. You can also bring topical words such as 'lottery' into play, as in:

They're a winning ticket in the eating lottery

You will find more of these examples listed under Apt, in the next chapter, together with a variety of different styles for you to choose from. Certainly food for thought !

CHAPTER EIGHT
Simply Slogans

Putting on the Style

In this chapter we now take a look at other styles of tiebreakers, which you may consider using for your entries.

Abbreviations

When you read competition rules, it normally says 'complete the tiebreaker sentence in not more than ten **words**'. So should I wish to say, 'I buy them for 4 good reasons', it is a simple matter to write the number 4 as the word, four. So what about abbreviations? They are not actual words but often there are no guidelines given in the rules. Well, I will leave you to decide whether you should use abbreviations or not, but I can tell you some very good entries have not only reached the judging table but won some major prizes too. Here are a few examples:

>AM PM 99 MM
>Even a harassed mum like me is made to feel a VIP
>Fairy Godmother - you - me QE2 - QED
>I can hog the BBQ without being a boar
>I can't get enough of the stuff - D' you C?
>It's the E - Z way to prevent D - K
>MPH, MPG, XR3, OK4 ME

Acronyms

An acronym is a word formed from the initial letters of another word. Winners have used product names, promoters names or other words apt to the contest, as in:

>Availability of No-nonsense Discounters Reflects Economic X'cellence
>Boots Offer Opportunities To Save
>Canada Affords Natural And Delightful Attractions
>Cheese Has Essential Elements Specially Emmental from Switzerland
>Delicious, A Nutritious Idea Sizzling Hot
>It's Cool And Neat And Downs A treat
>Perfect Ambience, Romantic Interludes, Sensational Paris
>Plants Excel And Truly Flourish in Rich Earthy Excellence
>Such Outstanding Delightful Amazing Perfection spells Sodap
>Terrific Exciting Considerate Superb Overwhelming

Chapter Eight : Simply Slogans

Adaptation

There are many phrases, clichés, proverbs, song titles, movie titles, etc., which can lend themselves to adaptation for use in tiebreakers. It pays to keep up with current events, noting when new films appear, new books published or people in the limelight. You can even gain ideas whilst watching television by noting well known catch phrases. The following are some examples, which may give you ideas on how to adapt topical phrases for future use:

Adapting books

Beyond our Great Ex - spud - tations
By Dickens, they Pip all other Great Expectations
It's First Amongst Sequels
It's huffed, it's puffed and we still wolf it down
Lorna - it never lets me Doone

Adapting catch phrases

Come on down, (product)'s price is right
I'm 'Alwight' like Michael Barrymore, 'cos (store)'s prices let me carry-more
I've started so ale finish
Plate it again, Sam
Steam me up Scottie

Adapting currency

Franc-ly, it's a capital place to be
I've a yen for travelling
Let's be franc, to win a trip would be my Arc de Triomphe
Mark my word, it's a capital place to be
To be 'franc' the very thought of it perks me up
Such super speed, stylish flair, will transform dad into a sterling millionaire

Adapting famous names

'Anne' excellent lager, to be 'Frank', the finest one I ever drank
Cleopatra found they did please her, their delicious taste made Julius 'Caesar'
Cuts through limescale, shine with ease, has the strength of Hercules
Forget Hanks, Costner and Swayze, my (product) would drive the ladies crazy
Fresh and sweet in jeans or nightie, I feel seductive as Aphrodite
It gives a sarnie more muscle than Arnie
Leconte get Becker for the Cash
Like Harlem Globetrotters they both go to great lengths for us shoppers
Nigel Mansell would lap it up
Shakespeare once said, a phrase to coin, my love 'Hath-a-way' with tenderloin

Adapting film titles

Born free, it's the taste that captivates
For effective cleansing without irritation, 'Annie' gets your gunge !
From Here to Maternity
Natal Attraction
Product's deodorant keeps me fresh in steamy encounters and fatal attractions
Whether jetting the world or 'home alone', it's up to the minute in any time zone

Adapting foreign words or names

Bon appetit ! bon voyage ! ?
Delicious mushroom, tasty cheese, my family parlez'more mum, please
'Eau' la la naturally, 'water' lot there is to see
'Francly' it's time I had something to 'brag-uette' about
I would be 'in-seine' not to try and win one
They would be trés cordiale, trés gentillé

Adapting place names

America's finest brings satisfied smiles at (store), best of the British Aisles
As-I-am shortly walking down the aisle this would 'Thai' the knot in style
It could send me totally Bahamas!
It puts 'US' in a 'State' of euphoria
My boots are made for New Yorking
No Thai-some scene, it reigns supreme
'O-Cay-man', I'll visit St. Lu. if 'Ja-maic-a' dream come true

Adapting product names

A Cloverly way to spread the family budget
'Eau' to be 'Schwepped' off my feet - C'est magnifiqué !
It's an Amiga sum to pay
It Raleighs to my assistance to lubricate resistance
It's gentle but tough, reliable too, A-riel winner through and through
Italian cuisine, gourmet selection, (product) is 'Clio-ly' perfection

Adapting proverbs

Many oils make bike work
Once fried, never forgotten
One good round deserves another
One good turn preserves another
Reflections speak louder than words
They make grape minds think, I like

Chapter Eight : Simply Slogans

Adapting sayings

All wise men are guided by these stars
Dataday, it gives us energy to work and play
It's the pork of the town from a store of renown
It's the taste that launched a thousand dips
Life's too short to rant and shave
The sun always rises in the yeast
They're signed, sealed and delicious
This tasty (product) is a stunner, one swallow does make a summer

Adapting songs

Every bunny, loves some bunny, sometimes
Flawless results, no tangle, no curl, perfection for 90's Material Girl
It would be 'Madness' to go anywhere else to furnish 'Our House'
On my island in the Sun (product) is my number one
(Product) is a girl's best friend
The answer my friend is glowing in the wind
Their popularity has greatly grown, with (product) you'll never walk alone
Wheel meat a gem

Adapting store names

Authentic tastes for us to savour, the 'Safeway' to exotic flavour
I'm a Co-optimist longing for a sip of sun
It Asda be one in a million
You'll Kwikly Save here

Adapting television and movie characters

Every can's - super man
I have always wanted to meet the loan arranger and silver
They're mission is to boldy go lower than any price has gone before
Together they are the dynamic duo, the 'canned crusader' and 'buy wonders'
Unlike Captain Kirk I can boldly go because (promoter) has gone before

Adapting television programmes

After stylish 5th Avenue - top for the shops, tantalising (product) is 'top of the pops'
It's the perfect plot on the landscape
It gently moves in ever 'degreasing' circles
Perfect meals in every way, come with 'the darling spuds of May'
Surprise ! Surprise ! this super selection is pure perfection
They are both 'Top of the s-hops'
Those darling spuds of May (and June) remind me of my honeymoon !

Adverts

I must admit in my pre-comping days, when the adverts came on television, it was a welcome break to put the kettle on. Now, I like to watch them. I wonder if you have noticed how many advertisement slogans are apt and witty, full of praise, or have a play on words. Whichever style is adopted, one important point is common to most - slogans are written in just a few words. Take a moment to reflect on a few; a famous slogan which is an excellent example is: Beanz Meanz Heinz - just three short words. One competition winner certainly took notice of advertisements and used the scenario to good effect, when he or she penned:

Whatever the journey, whatever the road - Perrier

Or how about:

If he left without a kiss, my consolation, chocolate bliss
Adventure reaches the parts everyday life cannot

Now many compers will be familiar with the chestnut, 'It reigns when it pours'. I was interested then, to read a tyre company's advertisement in a magazine: 'When it pours - we reign'.

Alliteration

After play on words, alliteration is a favourite style of tiebreaker writing. This is the art of writing a few words with the same initial letter. It need not extend to the entire tiebreaker, but may be confined to just a small section. Alliterative phrases are often used with other styles, for example, play on words and rhyme. The following are examples from which you may gain inspiration:

Absolutely ace, there I rest my case !
Baskets brimming with branded bargain buys
Carefully balanced, expertly blended, the building blocks nature intended
Chocolate casserole and chilli sauce are blasted away with equal force
Cool and clear, sweet or dry, a sparkling sensation, a superb buy
Designer china sets the scene, (product) protects and keeps it clean
Expertise plus elegance equals excellence
For family meals or haute cuisine, this trusted twosome reign supreme
From bumper to bumper, beginning to end, the (product) is the family's friend
From pole to pole it's your passport to problem-free purchasing
It's efficient, effective and environmentally friendly
It's superbly spreadable and gorge-ously edible
Nothing beats bubbly (product) whilst basking on Barbados beaches
Picked, prepared and packed at perfection, removes uncertainty from selection
Pocket the pennies for Italian break, spaghetti, vino and a pizza cake
Soup, savouries, sweets and sauce, (store) and (product) provide every course
They're picked, packed and purchased, post-haste

Chapter Eight : Simply Slogans

Amusing

When you consider judges frequently look through hundreds of similar sounding tiebreakers, how refreshing it must be to pause a while and read something which is different, or better still, makes them smile. The sentence doesn't need to be hilariously funny, and whatever you do, please keep your compilations printable.

Sometimes promoters ask entrants to write their tiebreakers in an 'apt and amusing manner' and this may cause some confusion. Do they mean amusing, as in funny, you may wonder, or do they simply mean a play on words. Now I can't give you the answer, because no-one knows just what the judges are looking for. Each contest is different and therefore the judging criteria will be too. All I can advise you to do is to study previous winning tiebreakers from the same promoters to glean some idea of what went before, as in:

> As Count Dracula said, one bite is enough to waken the dead
> Cleopatra found it did please her, her tenderloin made Julius Caesar
> It turns my frown upside down
> It's gammonteed to put a smile on your chops
> Josephine finally got it right, when she gave Napoleon (product) every night
> The garage guidance council recommend it, for pouring oil on troubled quarters
> When us couch potatoes outgrow our jackets, I need some (product) in tins or packets
> You can't beat drumsticks out of doors (barbecue theme)
>
> My ideal Concorde conversation during my flight on the world's only supersonic passenger aircraft would be...
> How Concorde is long in the nose, with plenty of body, silky smooth and distinctive - the aeroplane isn't bad either !

Apt

Now there's an interesting word. Just what does it convey to you in terms of writing tiebreakers? Apt, basically means using words which have some relevance to either the product, store, prize or theme of the contest. To take this to its extreme, if the contest is for a detergent with cutlery as the prize, then you should give your tiebreaker some apt words, for example:

> With (detergent)'s exclusive protection pledge, (promoter)'s cutlery has the edge

Note too, this example includes alliteration. Here are other apt ideas you may wish to consider:

> An excellent watch, second to none, all it's clocked up to be, time honoured fun
> Closer financial inspection proved interest-ing
> Great vibes are amplified, when music and (product) coincide
> Have a clutch of manifold advantages from a great distributor
> It cures an over developed thirst in a flash
> It helps make slimming a piece of cake !

Chestnuts

It may be arguable that chestnuts shouldn't be in this chapter at all. Chestnuts certainly aren't a style of slogan, but the word has been used so often in comping circles, that it has become a 'style' in a way.

A chestnut, is a tiebreaker which has been plagiarised time and again, perhaps with one or two words changed, but yet still continues to win major prizes. Some beginners to comping write 'chestnuts' completely innocently, unaware that their own original idea has been used before. Then there are other compers who quite blatantly copy previous winning tiebreakers, whether chestnuts or otherwise, submitting them as 'their own work'. This practice is frowned on by the majority of compers. Nothing is more annoying than having spent hours working on an apt and original entry, only to find, once the winners list has been circulated, that yet another chestnut has won again. Chestnuts do vary slightly, with a different word here and there, to fit the current comp, as in:

Delightfully exciting

Already struck lucky with (store)'s shopping, please (promoter) send me island hopping
(Location) excites me, shopping delights me, hope (promoter) invites me
(Product) delights me, the (location) excites me, hope (promoter) invites me
(Product) sipped at leisure, a fabulous (location) holiday pleasure

Expert perfectionist

Experts perfect it, perfectionists select it
Expert selection, matured to perfection, traditional criteria for (product) that's superior
Specialists perfect them, connoisseurs select them
(Store) has the best selection, whilst (product)'s freshness is perfection
Whilst nature selected the best, (product) perfected the rest

Family occasions

Family lunch or gourmet dinner, (product)'s always a winner
Family party or intimate liaison, (product) fits any occasion
For family protection, at little expense, (product) makes common sense
It's our favourite (product), tasty, nutritious, unbeatable value and quite delicious
Selected matured and guaranteed, for a snack, lunch, dinner or gourmet feed

I wanna be

Forty and naughty, not fifty and thrifty
I want to be like (film star) in suspenders, not (Pauline or Pat) in Eastenders
Instead of looking like (Pauline or Pat) in Eastenders, I want to resemble (supermodel) in suspenders

Chapter Eight : Simply Slogans 55

Polished performance

On reflection, they're sheer perfection
(Product)'s performance is second to none, just like (store), my number one
(Product) and (store) reign supreme, setting standards seldom seen

Reigns when it pours

It makes life richer for the pourer
This natural health restorer makes life richer for the pourer
With (product) life's richer for the pourer, (store) is the value scorer

Simply the best

Deliciously simple, simply delicious, (product) is versatile and nutritious
Exotic flavours, great selection, best ever, pure perfection
Juicy, tasty, full of zest, (product) are the best !

Tastefully done

Delicious, nutritious, wholesome (product), won't cost 'a packet' at (store)'s store
Tasty, healthy and nutritious, a cheap convenient food that's naturally delicious
The taste once acquired is forever desired

Thirst class team

It's 'thirst' come, 'thirst' served
They make a 'thirst' class team, quality and value score supreme
They make life richer for pourer, better for thirst

Unwavering standards

It's thirst quenching qualities never waver, first for value, first for flavour
(Store)'s standards of value never waver, (product) strike gold with chocolate flavour
Their standards never waver, first for value, first for flavour
Together their standards never waver, first for value, thirst for flavour
When quality and performance are a must, (product) and (store) are names you
can trust

Winning Team

For a Caribbean dream, (product) and (store) are the winning team
(Product) and (store) ensure this winning team, makes my (household items)
really gleam
Quality and value reign supreme, together they make a winning team

Coined Words

Coined words are those which have been made up from either fusing two words together, making a slight change to an existing word or other amendments, to arrive at a new and apt word. Here are some for win-spiration, which have won their author's prizes:

DIY with (product) is easy with their expert-ease
I can-a-letto myself choose without going pasta my limit
It's pure skindulgence
It's purr-fect purr-formance
It's simply sizzlicious
It gives fantastick results
It's Frenchsational
More smileage per gallon
We're chewsy

Colours

The use of colours, although not a very popular style, has appeared on winners lists, particularly when the theme has been environmentally 'green'. A few examples are:

Each is a red and green thirst-quenching machine
From the famous sign of green and white, my clothes return clean and bright
I was in the red, now I'm in the pink, so please leave me marooned !
It keeps the blues at bay, cosseted the (location)'s way
Pleasing little number in red and white, revealing a delightful bite
With brighter colours and whiter whites, my washday blues become green delights

Comparisons

This style is rather similar to praise, except instead of making a simple 'praise-the-product' phrase, you compare it to some-one or something else, for example:

Dolphins are joyful, safe and free, they're everything (product) allows woman to be
Like me, it's brilliant, robust, attractive, uncomplicated and nice to mix with

Compass

This style hasn't appeared on recent winners lists for quite sometime now, but was previously popular, as in:

North, East, South or West, (product)'s flavour is always best

Chapter Eight : Simply Slogans

Complements

Some tiebreaker slogans may ask you to say why a particular wine complements a certain kind of cuisine and you may find the following examples useful illustrations:

It's refreshing accompaniment for hot vindaloo, cooler than cucumber, tastier too !
Italian wine should be served with Bistecca alla florentina, moonlight and a signorina
Lunch al fresco, wurst with rye, tastes wunderbar with (product)'s dry (wine)
Sensational wine deserves mouth-watering food, chicken glazed in honey and barbecued
Steak au Poivré and French bread, complement this earthy red

Contrast

A style which has featured many times on winners lists, used either on its own or with a play on words, as you will see from these examples:

Four exotic flavours to savour, (product) doubles the taste, halves the labour
High quality and low prices go hand in hand
It's hard on dirt and soft on your purse
Style is neat from head to feet
They end a good meal and start a great conversation
They combine old-world courtesy with computer-age efficiency
With a (product) start, I get a brilliant finish

Conversation

Some competitions call for entrants to say who they would like to talk to and why, as in:

Charlie Chaplin
He'd find his hair would curl, when driven by this (product) girl
Sir Edmund Hilary
We could chat about a-scent that changed our life style
Timothy Dalton
007 like my (car), is handsome, reliable and can handle rough corners

Dialects

Being a Yorkshire lass, my own county has some wonderful sayings and the use of dialects in winning tiebreakers can make interesting and prizewinning reading:

Canny birds at (store)'s get fuller beaks, smaller bills
Ee by gum, I love 'taste !

Environmental Issues

A topical subject, which can be used to winning effect:

> Both are designed with the environment in mind
> Conserving nature and preserving beauty, buying (product) means pleasure with duty
> Energy saving, it's very green, my clothes and conscience would be clean
> Grand Canyon to tiny pore, (product) respects nature's law
> It's tender and kind, and keeps nature in mind
> It proves beauty doesn't have to cost the Earth
> (Store) teamed with (product)'s technology, saves on cash, supports ecology
> Traditional farming methods ensures (store)'s (product) is supreme
> Washing efficiency would be my intent, whilst doing loads for the environment

Generations

When you bring generation into play, it immediately establishes trust in a product or store. After all, a service or reputation cannot last throughout the generations unless it has stood the test of time. You may find it useful to note when anniversaries occur, and utilise this in your entries.

Since I have been entering competitions I have noticed that when a store or product reaches a milestone, they often launch a competition by way of bringing the public's attention to the event and perhaps to celebrate their continued good fortune with their customers.

> For twenty years this reliable friend, gives good value with less to spend
> From teens to thirties, journey's end, (product) remains a constant friend
> Grandpa loved them, so did dad, now they're favourites with the lad
> It's enjoyed from babies first tooth 'til grannies last
> Mum used it, grandma too, see the results and so will you
> Over sixty years in the baking and they're still going strong
> The quality never fades, even after ten decades
> The spread of the nation for the new generation

Inversion

I wonder if you remember the saying 'One for all and all for one'. This is a classic example of inversion, and a style which is little used, but can be quite effective, as in:

> Exactly 'write', to write exactly
> It's cleaning power is a powerful cleaner
> Quick off the mark for removing marks, quick
> Simply reliable, reliably simple
> We're crackers on (product) when it's (product) on crackers

Chapter Eight : Simply Slogans

Involvement

When writing tiebreakers, there are times when you can 'paint a picture' or set a scene. You may feel you are writing about a product you have just tried or a movie you have just watched, which was so involved, you thought you were there:

> It combines carnival, excitement, memories to last, spirit of the future, magic of the past
> It describes (location) with passion and flair, I was so involved, I thought I was there
> The excitement doesn't stop for a minute, I got so carried away, I thought I was in it

In Words

Newsworthy events are topical and can be included in tiebreakers. So too, can new words:

> Discovered the ketchup with mega appeal, it adds byte to every meal
> It gives your bread street cred
> Feel-good factor is finally found, with (product), the most comforting (item) around

Keep It Simple

Some tiebreakers seem to go on, and on and on. Most of the words are superfluous and a quick snip here and there can do wonders. One of the secrets of writing winning tiebreakers is - Kiss, which stands for: Keep It Simple, Short. Simply say what the product does for you or how the service is of benefit, as in:

> Hot from the hob with a buttery knob, they're just the job !
> In a wok, (product) sizzles with international flavour
> Melt the cube, release the flavour, delicious stir fries, ready to savour
> To use, they're simplicity, their flavours, authenticity

Limericks

Another version of the amusing style. A limerick consists of five lines. The first two lines and the last line all rhyme with each other. Lines three and four rhyme with each other, but not with the other lines, and are much shorter in length. Normally, entrants are asked to complete the last three lines or the last line to a given limerick, as in:

> A fruit split with a texture of cream
> Could send you on your holiday dream
> What could be better
> Than this holiday mecca
> Served up with a fruity supreme

Long Established

This is a similar style to generation, but rather than ponder on the 'grandad, dad and now lad' theme, the emphasis is on long established trading, as in:

>From a great past comes a perfect present
>Quality and value never date, their service you can still appreciate
>Three centuries of expertise, qualities and value which are sure to please

Mathematics

A limited style, but one which could prove useful when the contest has a numerical theme:

>I am one hundred 'per scent' sure of exuding feminine allure
>(Product) all adds up to tasty meals, subtracting pounds with their super deals

Memories

When the prize holiday on offer is to an interesting place or somewhere from which you would bring back fond memories, you may like to incorporate this into your entries, as in:

>A nappy clad bottom which wiggles, must be filmed for future giggles
>Camcorder memories show days gone by, when (product) kept my babies dry
>This cool delicious fortified sensation ensures a perfect memorable vacation

Mottoes

Who, I wonder can remember the famous words from Julius Caesar:

>Veni, vidi, vici - I came, I saw, I conquered

This was adapted for use in a frozen food contest, winning its author a Concorde flight, as in:

>They came, they thaw, they Concorde the market

Mouthwatering

You can make your entries stand out, if you make the judges feel as though they can actually taste the product or see a place as though they were actually there, as in:

>Orange and lime from tropical clime, glow with the hues of exotic views

Chapter Eight : Simply Slogans

Names

Some tiebreakers call for entrants to submit a name for a sandwich, car, hot air balloon, jumbo jet etc., as in:

Name a sandwich

Farmhouse feast
Four star filler
Hamapple hunk
Hamazon
Healthy stacker
High Riser
Munchosaurus
Silencer
Triple treasure

Name a hot air balloon

Above all
Air of distinction
Bubble over
Fizzible difference
Pop pop and away
S-up, s-ip, and away

Name a car

Applause	It goes like the clappers
Axminster	It would be my little car pet
Bo Peep	It's a little beauty under the bonnet
Graduate	It has a degree of distinction
Ingot	It's worth its weight in gold
Iris	An absolute eye opener
Jade	Everyone else just turns green with envy
Mousetrap	It's a long running success
Soda pop	A little gas gives it a lot of fizz
Top Gun	Its the car I'd love to Cruise with

Name a jumbo jet

Plain contentment (chocolate product)

Negatives

This is a style I dislike, as I prefer to make positive statements when writing my tiebreakers. However, it has certainly gained favour with judges, as these have all appeared on winners lists:

I'm a worse 'sight' off without them
They knock spots off rivals
Whatever happens, we don't get 'cheesed-off' with (product)
When games over it's never 'tough cheddar' with (product)

Nostalgia

This style is similar in a way to generation, but gives the reader pause for thought, as in:

> Delicious treat shared my passion, when (product)'s sweeties were on ration
> It bridges the generation gap, golden oldies at prices way back
> Nostalgia glows from (store)'s aisles, old fashioned prices, sweetest smiles

Numbers

When I mentioned abbreviations, I pointed out that strictly speaking these aren't words. The same applies to numbers but with one distinct different, you can write numbers as words, for example, 20 becomes twenty. There are instances though, where writing them as words would be a disadvantage, for example:

> 2,4,6,8 (product)'s beers, at (store)'s prices, we say 'cheers'

It really all boils down to a personal preference. Here are a few more:

> 4 me 2 B in GTE, XL's I buy 2 smoke U C
> It gives 1001 ways to please your tastebuds
> It makes the 19th hole the one I like the best
> (Store) display their a b c's and 1,2,3's, making sure each partnership agrees
> They're wanted by the FBI - Fruity Bun Indulgers
> This recipe, tastes like heaven, dating back to '37

Partnerships

When you collect entry forms from supermarkets, you will find they feature a specific product, for example, cheese. You may then be asked to say why you bought the cheese from this particular store. Other times, the 'partnership' may consist of the store, product and the company who are awarding the prize, for example, a car manufacturer.

Given that most entries have to be written in under fifteen words, and many compers do like to mention the promoter's names, you could very well end up with a tiebreaker consisting mainly of names. To overcome this, you may like to find some common denominator which can be applied to all members of the 'partnership'. The following are a variety which may give you food for thought:

> On reflection, these partners in shine, give sparkling service, time after time
> This team has the winning theme, value, quality and service
> This winning team grew to fame by putting quality behind their name
> Together they're a team to savour, one for value, one for flavour
> Together they're a winning team, a passport to my American dream

Chapter Eight : Simply Slogans

Please, Please Take Me !

A 'plane' old plea to the judges, 'will you please take me on this prize holiday', as in:

Fun, entertainment, a different place, please save us a place!
Housewife, mother, going insane, please take me on this train
(Product)'s food is unsurpassed, thanks to (promoter), I'm packing fast
(Product) you'd have my thanks if I could go and spend your francs
The wine stock's low and so's the cheese, can we go to France please?

Praise

Everyone of us likes to hear words of thanks or encouragement. It makes us feel good. So why not praise a product you like or the service you receive in a store. A word of caution though, please don't overdo it when writing tiebreakers. Although promoters like to hear good things about their products, you could hardly blame them for being sceptical if you lavish praise by the 'dollop load' as they say in Yorkshire. The following are examples of praise for the product, praise for the store and praise for both:

Praising the product

Best value is always underlined but quality never undermined
It's their logo recognised everywhere, a promise of value and quality care
Sparkling results every time, it gives my sinks a lasting shine
The finest foods tastefully canned, excellent prices and service grand
Their skill in authentic spice blending, means flavour never requires amending
They've found the formula to succeed, unbeatable performance is guaranteed

Praising the store

Branded quality, money savers, customer care, that never wavers
Each receipt defies defeat, their prices are never beat
Highest quality, lowest price, helpful staff, are really nice
Own label, names renowned, greatest choice, best prices around
Quality's excellent, prices right, choice extensive and service bright
Shoppers haven, prices fair, excellent quality and customer care

Praising the product and store

Both products and store ensure bargains galore
For price, quality, convenience and speed, they both have everything I need
(Product) and (store), you'll observe, are inviting, welcoming and quick to serve
(Product) has conquered stain removal, and (store)'s prices win shoppers approval
Quality and value equally shared, (store) and (product) are perfectly paired
The range is vast, the service fast, with taste and value unsurpassed

Product Knowledge

Just as you may feel a milestone in a company or product's history is worth mentioning in your entries, you may feel some knowledge you have gained, through reading their advertising literature, may prove to be prizewinning too, as in:

> My excuse to eat more chocs, is forty million Lego blocks

Problem Solving

You may have written tiebreakers praising the product and have mentioned such generalised words as, quality, value, choice etc. You could extend this idea further, by simply stating you buy this product because it solves your problems.

Maybe, like me, your DIY leaves much to be desired. Give me a tube of glue and I get more on myself than on what I'm supposed to be sticking. Therefore, I would never ever dare use superglue. I would probably spend the next few hours at the casualty department, explaining why a china cat I was gluing together was stuck firmly to my arm !

So when an adhesive manufacturer brought out a new kind of 'idiot proof' nozzle, this solved my problem. I can now use superglue with confidence. Well, alright ! A bit more confidence. Now, I've only half a cat stuck to my arm !

Should you find a product solves your problems, then why not tell the promoter, as in:

> Day or night, whatever the hour, turn the key, release the power
> It does the trick by sealing the brick
> It solves problems life produces with its multitude of uses
> Protective, moisturising, preservative free, I'd feel the difference others can see
> Solutions to weighty problems I'd surely find for just the figure I had in mind
> What was a chore, now allows time for so much more

Repetition

This style can be seen on winners list, although it's not a style which is used too frequently. Repetition is useful when you want to make a specific point and then hammer it home or merely just to emphasis the statement, as in:

> A classic car deserves a classic sound system
> A fitting name for a fitting garment
> Easy to use, easy to clean, easily the best for great cuisine
> Four great flavours, four star treat, for lower prices, impossible to beat
> It censors waste, it censors grime, a (product) wash every time
> Simply reliable, reliably simple

Chapter Eight : Simply Slogans

Sentiment

When competitions have a romantic theme, you may like to use a little sentiment, as in:

> An old romantic who loves his wife, longs to fulfil the dream of her life
> I would give it to my special mum
> Just been picturing bygone times, funny to imagine life without (product)

Sharing

Entrants may be asked to say who they would share a specific product with and why, as in this example of sharing sandwiches:

> Addams family   There's no tastier bite, for a 'monster' appetite
> Jean Bott   She is popular and always stars in bread
> Stephen Hendry   He's always ready for a break
> The Gladiators   They would 'wolf' it down like 'lightning'

Similarity

This style is similar to repetition. However, instead of repeating words, here the use of two similar sounding words come into play, as in:

> A little simmer brings out the summer
> It's healthy and hearty and great for a party
> It means survival and revival for whatever's thrown in
> Their brightening and whitening is guaranteed

Staccato

This style of tiebreaker makes effective use of short, sharp words, as in:

> Breakfast, brunch, lunches, dinner, it tastes so nice, (product)'s a winner
> Hygienic, powerful, cleansing, quick, it's multi-cleaning span is spick !
> Keywords (store)'s shoppers learn, enter, select, save, return
> Oranges, Mint, Raisins, Sultanas, temptation inside drives me Bahamas

The winner of *Intacomps* Win A Competition Package contest, used this effect when completing the sentence: I love comping because...

> Car ! Holiday ! Cash ! Possession ! Forget the love, make that obsession !
> I know the feeling !

Sympathy

This style has appeared on winners lists, but I must admit is one I've never used. I prefer to be positive with my entries, rather than hoping to win because I've gained the judges' sympathy. However, this is my own personal viewpoint, and some entrants have met with success using this style, as in these examples:

> Gloomy nights, recession bites, taste of (product) sees me right !
> Mother of four is no joke, jaded, harassed, constantly broke
> Mum's break from routine is overdue, shopping trip would be a dream come true
> Spirits low, finances chronic, (location) is the perfect tonic
> Tired of mundane (town)'s shopping, would love to do some channel hopping

Topicality

Now this is one style in which you can excel, just by keeping up with the news, latest films and topical events. Now some events occur regularly each year - Christmas, Easter, New Year, The Budget, Wimbledon, sports championships. So should you be sending in entries with a 31 December closing date, you could include either a Christmas theme or a New Year Resolution. I won a prize to a luxury health and country club, when I mentioned:

> It would `fit' my New Year Resolution

Another topical event, and one which promoters always organise competitions for, is the Olympics. So if you mention sportsmen or women in your tiebreaker, then do ensure you are right up to date with sporting events.

Some newsworthy events may give you ideas for tiebreakers, but there is always the danger that by the time your entry has been judged, perhaps two months later, the event will have been forgotten. However, that's a chance you have to take, so should multiple entries be allowed, you may like to send in one topical tiebreaker and another one with a completely different style. How about these for inspiration:

Christmas and New Year

> Authentic taste and unique location, guarantee a truly festive occasion
> Be a thrill with stockings to fill, Christmas shopping, and not paying the bill
> To choose priceless gifts from a sparkling display would keep me happy 'till Hogmanay

Elections

> As the Chancellor panics and changes his plans, your money at least is in capable hands
> In the wise 'buy' election, it's the greatest selection
> When set before the house, it gets an all party vote

Chapter Eight : Simply Slogans

Health

It spreads with ease and contains no E's
Juicy, sweet and full of vitamin C, for a healthy lifestyle (product) is the key
There's nothing added, nothing removed, (product) cannot be improved

National Lottery

Forget the lottery, this'll do fine to guarantee a winning line

News Items

What's Royal gets Eton

Well, this was a news item when I wrote it down. See what I mean !

Trust

A similar style to praise, but this time the emphasis is on why you feel you can trust the promoter, as in:

Busy housewives demand the best, these trusted names ensure success
Everywhere that germs are lurking, mums trust (product) to go on working
It's the brand I can trust when lasting protection is a must
Tried and tested, found to be true, dependable friend, delicate hue
Where quality and value are a must, (product)'s the one to trust

Value For Money

Some tiebreakers include the price of the product for comparison, as in:

Both make perfect sense to me, avoiding hassle for 13p
I could inherit Aphrodite's beauty for as little as five pounds, ninety five pence
Of unbeatable quality and sunshine only costing two 99
Prizewinning biscuits, lucky me, a Caribbean holiday for sixty two p
Springtime freshness for thirteen pence, like shopping at (store) makes common sense

Visit

Some competitions will ask you to say who you would take with you on a trip, who you would make a phone call to, where you would like to ride your new mountain bike or even where you would eat your sandwiches. There are several variations on the object, people or place theme as you will see in the following examples:

Visit cinema to see

Cats	It's purr-fect entertainment
Cats	No other show comes within a whisker of it
Midsummer Nights Dream	Too many chocolates and I'm all 'Bottom'
Phantom of the Opera	Two's company, three's a shroud
South Pacific	Its nautical but nice !
Starlight Express	From 'best box', you can 'chew chew' your way through favourite chocs

Visit health club with

Boss	No deadlines, targets, phones or fax, trimmed, slimmed and pampered, we'd both relax
Calculator	I'd work out with multipled vigour, change vital statistics and round down my figure
Doctor	Forget depression, don't need the pills, this relaxing break will cure my ills
Friend	You rest and relax and exercise too, improve your appearance, create a new you
Husband	Harassed house husband under pressure, needs indulgence, rest and leisure
Husband	To be transformed from Jeeves into Wooster would give his morale a real booster
Mirror	Being pampered to perfection, I'd gladly look at my radiant reflection
Psychiatrist	It's the perfect location for a shrink
Sister	There they could take the `L' out of flab, leaving us looking absolutely fab
Spare tyre	I could leave it behind as a thank you present

Visit objects

Every kid's lunch box	Kids need varied food that's nutritious, (product)'s are that and they're delicious
My plate	They're easy to eat but hard to beat
My school	Dished daily for school dinners, (product) are certain winners
My sports bag	When it comes to crunch, there's no better munch

Visit people

Sherlock Holmes	I've always wanted to visit the Ideal Holmes Exhibition
Bank Manager	It would prove I can balance (cycle prize)
Dentist	Something I'd give my eye-teeth for
Captain Kirk	I'd like to take him where no man has gone before

Chapter Eight : Simply Slogans

Visit places

A football stadium	Rival supporters home and away unite for a (product) the (promoter)'s way
Amsterdam	Let's face it my solitaire deserves a perfect setting
Ben Nevis	I want my fitness to reach a peak
Bottle banks	Because I like to get things recycled
Health Club	Because no more spare tyres for this bicycle belle
Norway	It's the only way I can a fjord to travel
Smithfield Market	Everyone would want a butchers at my (prize)
Speakers Corner	It's the best place to hold a Raleigh
Stock Exchange	I want to be a big wheel in the city
Swish restaurant	Because at 16 I can't handle bars
Town	It would be a honey in the jams

Word Association

This is not a style you will see frequenting winners lists, but does have its possibilities, as in:

If the world's your oyster, (product) is the pearl

Words Within Words

This is an interesting style to use, and an alternative to using coined words, as in:

At (store), it's always `sav-oury' food
Driving authenticity home (promoter)'s `car-is-ma' pastaport to Rome
It affords a great oppor`tune'ity
(Product) spreads satisfaction with an everest-ing speedy action
Their flavour flows, past my head to-ma-toes
There's an a`bun'dance of bread
We're very `sell'ective

Prizewinning Ways

I am sure the styles in this chapter will provide you with several interesting ideas when writing your own tiebreakers. A source of reference you can refer to time and again.

As you browse through the tiebreakers in the next chapter, you will probably note the majority use rhyme with play on words, coined words and alliteration.

I wonder how many other different styles you will identify and use yourself in the future.

CHAPTER NINE
Prizewinning Slogans

Like many compers, you may like to look through lists of winning tiebreakers for inspiration when writing your own entries. New ideas and topical events, as well as revamped tiebreakers and chestnuts keep appearing, therefore you may be interested to note the types of tiebreakers which are currently catching the judge's eye.

Intaslogans

You will already have seen the lists of words and phrases in the *Intaslogans* series of booklets from the extracts in chapter two, and the advantages of using these effectively in chapter five. However, words and phrases in *Intaslogans* is only a small part, the main section of the booklets contain complete tiebreaker ideas, as shown in this chapter.

Prizewinning Slogans

You will appreciate new competitions are continually being promoted and reflect the changing judging trends. To provide compers with up-to-date lists, the *Prizewinning Slogans* series was launched in March 1995. These are in A4 size booklets, listed by products for easy reference, and follow the format shown in this chapter. There is also a useful cross reference section on the three most popular themes of motoring, sport and travel. *Prizewinning Slogans* booklets are published at six monthly intervals. The advantage, instead of publishing an annual volume, is to keep you up-to-date on the current judging scene.

So what is the difference between the tiebreakers in *Intaslogans* and *Prizewinning Slogans*.

Each *Intaslogans* booklet covers just one type of product or theme, e.g. *Intaslogans : Dairy* has tiebreakers for cheese, butter, spreads, yoghurt and cream, as shown in the extracts in this chapter under Food : Dairy.

Prizewinning Slogans covers a wide range of products from a variety of competitions, again as shown in this chapter.

BABYCARE

Babyfood, nappies, etc

A nappy clad bottom which wiggles, must be filmed for future giggles
Best for changing tender bots means I needn't tender lots
Busy mums, no time to spare, can rely on (product) for babycare
Camcorder memories show days gone by, when (product) kept my babies dry
Capturing smiles, memories so happy, a gurgling baby in his (product)'s nappy
Carefully balanced, expertly blended, the building blocks nature intended
Clear skies, blue sea, mummy, daddy and now there's me !
Day or night my baby's delight shows the (product)'s choice is right
For keeping my baby clean and content, (product) is money well spent
From medicines to feed, from bottom to top, everything they need is stocked in one shop
Happy babies, happy mums, bubbly baths and powdered bums
Healthy baby, happy days, buying (product) always pays
Home-made tastes, better than mine, purest ingredients, saves me time
I use (product) when only the best is bawled for
I'd have happy little faces and clean little places
Lots of choice, little waste, carefully selected with home-made taste
My baby offers love and affection (product) offers feeding perfection
One is bottom on prices, the other is priceless on bottoms
Other babies merely grow, but (product) babies steal the show
(Product) gives the finest care for baby wear
(Product) keeps baby dry and clean, (store) keeps prices very keen
(Product) starts your baby off on the right foot
Pure perfection for the young, natural goodness on the tongue

Safe, reliable, roomy and when won, will prove (store)'s lot is an'appy one !
Scrumptious baby food as nature intended, nutritious ingredients carefully blended
Soak up the splash without drying the cash
(Store) is tops for value and (product) is tops for botoms
(Store)'s value is the best, while (product)'s dryness beats the rest
(Store) has everything my baby needs under one roof at prices I can afford
Super absorbent, like a glove, (product) for the one you love
Tasty meals for hungry tums, tempt those little gourmet gums
Tempting varieties handy little pots, grown-up menus for tiny tots
The best ingredient selection, convenient jars of pure perfection
There's both nappies and toys, bringing mother and baby joys
They are specially designed with babies in mind
They give variety by the ladleful for kids by the cradleful
They pamper and care for necessities bare
They provide hours of play in a safe hygienic way
They soothe babies cares and troubles with silky talc and bubbly bubbles
They turn leisure into pleasure for my little treasure
They're a dynamic duo beyond compare, relied on for (product)'s babycare
They're brightly coloured and easy to hold, lots of fun for my one year old
They're the best that mummy can buy
They're the winning combination for the younger generation
When you're in the crawler lane you need the right gear
Wholesome pure and really nutritious, baby thinks it tastes delicious

CLEANSERS

Detergents, bleaches, polishes etc

A clean sweep would give me the brightest holiday

A dish-washing combo beyond compare is (store)'s value and (product)'s care

A little (product) ensures, this winning team makes my (household items) really gleam

(Appliance) does the hardest work (product) gets the dirtiest dirt

At this price I can go clean round the world

Beautiful craftsmanship, what a combination, when (product) protects such a gleaming reputation

Bright and shining, perfectly clean, (product) and (store) a winning team

CD brightness CD shine, (product)'s magic is all mine

Clean home, low price, Christmas dinner, that's nice (hamper prize)

Cleaning power is a must (store) and (product) are names to trust

Consistent results and sparkling performance is always considered of prime importance

Cutlery that gives a lifetime of pleasure retains its perfection with each (product) measure

Cuts through limescale, shine with ease, has the strength of Hercules

Designer china sets the scene, (product) protects and keeps it clean

Everywhere that germs are lurking mums trust (product) to keep on working

Finest china in English tradition, deserves (product) protect its condition

For a self catering break it's the ideal 'take'

For cleansing and bleaching their range is far reaching

For customer care there's none finer, kind on price, gentle on china

For gleaming results I'm very impressed, (product) outshines the rest

For savings, service, convenience and speed they both fulfil every housewife's need

Goodbye germs, goodbye infection, (product) gives me complete protection

Hard on limescale, smooth on hands, most effective on pots and pans

I always get perfection from the finest cleaning selection

In caravan, apartment, hotel, (product) at (store) serves me well

In my kitchen sink drama it's my knight in shining armour

It gently moves in ever 'degreasing' circles

It gives my dishes the perfect after dinner glint

It's a legend in its own grime

Its the best solution at the scene of the grime

Its the squirt that worries the dirt

Millions of housewives can't be wrong, product is thorough, clean and strong

More hygienic, powerful, quick, its multi-cleansing span is spick

Nothing beats this sparkling team for beautiful settings, spotlessly clean

On reflection these partners in shine give sparkling service, time after time

Outshines all rivals for choice

Pick up (product), give a squirt, say goodbye to germs and dirt

Powerful on sinks, saucepans too, a polished performance comes shining through

Quality ware and quality care, together they make the perfect pair

Quick off the mark for removing marks, quick

(Product)'s liquid is gentle in action, (store) prices give satisfaction

(Product)'s, name means in every sense, disinfectant excellence

(Product) cleans everywhere sparkling clean, for (store)'s value I'm always keen

(Product) conquered stain removal and (store)'s prices win shoppers approval

(Product) shifts grime, grease is busted, (store)'s name reliably trusted

Removes grease and smells so fresh, with (store)'s value a great success

Sparkling results every time, it gives my sinks a lasting shine

Chapter Nine : Prizewinning Slogans

CLOTHING

Fashion, design, etc

Affordable prices, luxury feel, (product) always has fashionable appeal

Any season, at all events, (product) inspire compliments

Arriving in style, dressed to kill, thanks to designer skill

Bike it or hike it with (store) I like it

Bronx to California, 'cut' for 'action' (product)'s 'star' gives 'premiere' satisfaction

Business pleasure here and there, quality and style beyond compare

Buy a (product) - imitation is the sincerest form of flattery

By stocking (product)'s sportswear, (store) know the score, converting me to (product No.2), keeps me running back for more

Classy car, classy clothes, make heads turn wherever she goes

Clothes for camping, skiing, hiking, (product)'s range is to my liking

Coast to coast, across the nations, fashionable style build great foundations

Comfort and style make travel worthwhile

Elegant, eye-catching effortless style, (product)'s clothes are perfectly cast

Extensive choice, helpful advice, lovely to wear, sensible price

Eye-catchingly chic, fashionable style, reliable and comfortable, mile after mile

For adventure, work or leisure, (product) gives lasting pleasure

For easy care, comfortable wear, they fit and shape with style and flair

For fashionable clothing unsurpassed, (product) are always perfectly cast

Forget Hanks, Costner and Swayze, my (product) would drive the ladies crazy

From rodeo to studio, (product)'s star quality steals the show

Gentle stroll, mountain hike, (store) have the clothes I like

Glamorous outfits greatly enhance, (product) guarantees an admiring glance

I could play the wild rover from Yorkshire to Dover

Legs look longer and slimmer when (product) softly shimmer

Luxurious and ultra light, elegantly dressy for that special night

Master tailoring at its best, (product) are a cut above the rest

Now the exclusive is not so elusive

On any location from France to Japan, (product) make the macho man

(Product) are `expressly orient'ated towards fashion and style

(Product) are one step ahead and a price rise behind

(Product) has glamour to view and fashion for you

Quality garments, classic design, the label is (product), the comfort is mine

Skirts and sweaters in cahoots, are joined by bonnets, sometimes boots

Style neat from head to feet

The ultimate in style and flair they suit the occasions anywhere

Their appearance can change together to adapt to any weather

Their range is extensive but never expensive

Their separates with designer chic, business or leisure creations unique

Their stylish quality, greatly admired, is always right, always desired

This authentic 'cut' my family adore, so (product) please 'take four'

Unbeatable quality, eye-catching style, travel triumphantly mile after mile

When style and fashion really matter, (product) will always flatter

Wide choice, helpful advice, quality products, sensible price

With authentic '(product)' western 'flair' I'd remember forever that 'I was there !'

You have drive and style, which stand out a mile

CONFECTIONERY

Sweets, chocolates, chews, etc

A contented car load makes light of the longest road

A weekend in Vienna, is my dream come true, a night at the opera and dinner for two, a ride in a carriage, the music of Strauss, then enjoying (product) in a quaint coffee house

Beside the Seine, we'd open the box, two lovers in love - with (product)'s chocs !

Both harbour special pleasure, sheer indulgence, times to treasure

Boutiques, bistros, Le Metro, Montmatre, like (product)'s assortment it's captured my heart

Capital idea, the city for lovers, whilst outside your window the man in black hovers

Delicious boxed assortments are magical treats the sky scrapers, cabs and numbered streets

Devouring elephant or bear, I'm quick to save the lion's share

Each fabled mountain peak is just like (product), totally unique

Freedom has an orange shape, perfect for a sweet escape

From every bar its fun to see animals emerge three by three

Galaxy of gifts, bounty of fun, a (store)'s treat is number one

Heights and sights, (product) too, would be a memorable Yankee do

Hilton? Let's not be pedantic, for (product) I'd swim the Atlantic

Hollywood, Disneyland, Frisco, LA - these dreams and (product) make mothers day

I always chews the best and (product) beat the rest

I always wolf them down so mum keeps a pack in reserve

I could get everything I long to play, just grab my trolley and chocs away

I enjoy (product) and (store) shopping, the extra temptation, Florida hopping

I'd go on a toy'riffic spree and thanks to (store) it would be free

If he left without a kiss, my consolation, chocolate bliss

It contains tails of the unexpected

Its a little taste of heaven that doesn't cost the earth

It's the longest lasting and has so many different flavours

Like a (promoter)'s ferry, it is transport of delight

My darling man deserves a treat, send us to Paris, tout suité!

My friends drool when I take (product) to school

My husband, romantic? absolutely never, a weekend in Paris could change him, forever

New York, (product), means chocs away, because my lady just loves Broadway

Nickels, dollars, pounds or pence, (product) at (store) makes good cents

No haste, just cool taste for a chewsy person

One little chew, makes me feel like new

Only (product)'s flavour lasts through English, French and into maths

Open your mouth wide enough and the animals enter three by three

Paris is sparkling, alive and alight, the way (product) makes me feel tonight

(Product), Paris, a ring and a rose - hope she'll accept when I propose

(Product), toys, games and mouth watering splendour, its my chance to be a big spender

(Promoter)'s car like (product)'s bar goes tastefully far

Rectangle, triangle or someTimes Square, (product) makes great New York fare

Rival products don't compete, Switzerland with (product), what a treat

(Store), (product) and Lady Luck could lead me straight to Donald Duck

The best by gum, beyond compare, flavours to savour anywhere

The happiest combination by far is a (promoter)'s trip plus (product)'s bar

Chapter Nine : Prizewinning Slogans 75

COSMETICS

Skincare, make-up, deodorants etc

Affordable protection, adds a glow to my complexion
Although saying 'goodbye' to make-up is what you seek, to be effective and gentle you could also add chic
Carefully cleansing, pampering pores, repairing the damage a wild life can cause
Continually evolving towards perfection, (product) is my natural selection
For personal care with flair, (product) pampers a girl beyond compare
Gentle protection, fragrances that enhance, guaranteeing freshness and many an admiring glance
Having tried the rest, my skin says (product) is best
I don't want to leave my appearance in the 'lap of the gods'
I feel, whatever the hour, I've just had a shower
I look clean, smell fresh and with (car) I'm bound to impress
I use it morning, noon and night for comfort and perfumed delight
I'd have no hair raising problems, only close shaves
I'm cool, collected in command, nice to know and in demand
Its fragrance, crisp and fresh, keeps me feeling at my best
Its gentle technique preserves beauty's mystique
Its kindness is worldwide
It's kind to skin, not animal tested, definitely money well invested
It's pure and gentle, fragrance free, kind to animals, perfect for me
It's selective, protective and extremely effective
It's so simple it keeps skin smooth without a dimple
It's superior selection, second to none, for cool confidence, number one
It's tender and kind, and keeps nature in mind
It 'Pandas' to my facial pores - and supports an even greater cause
It aids a slipping beauty
It gently enhances my complexion and helps encourage wildlife protection
Its gentle touch, always healing, soon restores that loving feeling
Its simple routine designed with care that keeps skin smooth and healthy beyond compare
Like a mother or best friend, on (product) you can depend
Motoring perfection on the move, (product) when the going gets smooth
Nature sometimes needs a little help
New York, Paris, London or Rome, (product)'s cosmetics are a class on their own
Precious skin needs loving care, cruelty free (product) is beyond compare
(Product) gently cleans dirt away, protecting the face of tomorrow, today
Pure and light, cleanses to perfection, leaves me with a glowing complexion
Reassuring and reliable makes me feel desirable
Signs of 'wildlife' belong only on the face of the Earth
Something old, something new, the spice of life, you know who
The beauty of (product) is pure face value
They're quality products, luxuriously chic, superior, modern and quite unique
Those luscious lips, he can't resist, will ensure your quarrel won't persist
To banish spots, grease and grime, I use (product) every time
Whatever the year, style or trend, (product) is always my best friend
With beauty only skin deep, (product) makes it mine to keep
With its secret power, it keeps me fresh hour after hour

DRINKS

Alcoholic

A good head with plenty of body always gets results !
A winning choice, but no intrigue, (store)'s savings are major league
After a mammoth shopping spree (product) is the perfect reviver for me
Best beer ! Best supplier about ! (product) and (store) - no drought !
(Product) 'cheers' the winning way - sip, sip, sip hooray !
Carefully poured, gently swirled it's the tastiest beer in the world
Consistent quality is what I seek, can after can, week after week
Drinking lager I adore, could win CD's from chart topping store
Elementary my dear (product), I always detect when something is brewing
Every can's - super man
Favourite store and a brew supreme, (product) and (store), what a team !
For quality, value, taste and tradition, (product) and (store) defy competition
Genuine value in bottle or cans, quality surpasses other brands
Handy to carry, low on price, tastefully canned, bottled and nice
Having tacked my first 'case' I could murder another
I enjoy a little light refreshment for 'time out' after shopping contentment
Its strength and style make taste buds roar, hopefully for an encore !
It's the one beer drinkers adore from the store that offers more
It's perfect brew, instant pleasure, lasting enjoyment simply beyond measure
Much better than other ales, random tests, it never fails
Other beers are less appealing, (product) guarantees that winning feeling
Superior brew, refreshing and strong. (store)'s price, can't go wrong

Non Alcoholic

A bedtime coffee at its best, leaves me feeling quite refreshed
A bite of (product), a sip of tea, that's paradise for me !
A cupful taken early morning helps to stop persistent yawning
A (product)'s reviver is great for every driver
Aromas excite, flavours delight, this medium roast always gets my breakfast toast
Arousing aroma, flavour diving, perfect product to rise and shine
As you rise and shine, the aroma's divine
Blenders of such superior tea would package India most successfully
Distinct refreshing morning cuppa, lifts at luncheon, soothes at supper
Every bag is full of flavour, rounding up a taste to savour
Expertly blended to taste sublime, perfect coffee every time
First for thirst, it's a sparkling disc-overy
Great taste, prize winning quencher, pull the ring for a (location) adventure
It perks me up and filters my cares away
Its fruity taste refreshes you mile after mile
It's one bottleneck I enjoy getting stuck in
Less to carry, less to store, less to pay, more to pour
Original, diet, caffeine free, I can't choose so I buy all three
Perfect flavours, cheerful smiles, super value, (product)'s style
(Product)'s classic tingle, makes movie magic multilingual
Sparkling (product), (location)'s sun, the quickest way to family fun
Splendid drink on which I thrive, also I can drink and drive
Tastes like juice, dilutes like squash
Tennis or 'squash' this partnership serves up the best
Their fizzy flavours will soon have your friends clutching at straws

Chapter Nine : Prizewinning Slogans

ELECTRICAL APPLIANCES

TV, video, satellite, fridge, iron etc

A delicious flavour, blends with ease, processed by (product), guaranteed to please
Astronomical savings, wide selection, tuned to get a good reception
Bargains that are always repeatable, means their 'system' is unbeatable
Bargains, offers, make me richer, value, service, completes the picture
Classy appliances, brand new wheels, (product) 'drive' the greatest deals
Convenient to my workplace, easily used and cleaned, performance, perfection, best seen
Dishing up a great selection, heavenly prices, best reception
Dynamic performance, hi-tech appliance, programmed for guaranteed reliance
Every (product) sold is worth its weight in gold
Every purchase without exception, always gets a great reception
Everything is programmed in, right down to the last bargain
Excellent ranges, quality supreme, price is low, a shoppers dream
Expertise plus elegance equals excellence
Fast forward viewing, (store) wins, fishical pleasure from (product)'s tins
For freezing, cooking, cleaning and dishes, (product) fulfils my wishes
For price and performance they are so cool
For prospects of audio visual perfection, explore (product)'s fantastic selection
For quality, craftsmanship, style and precision, (product) needs no revision
Frothier froth and instant steam, extract the best from the coffee bean
I buy (product) first to last, such quality and value is unsurpassed
I only mix in the best circles
Its o'fishall, (store) and (product) both have fine tuna's
Its spacious design eye-catching pleasing, plenty of room for cooling or freezing
Low priced quality, without exception, always gets a good reception
Never need to channel hop, (product)'s standards never drop
Prices are never off beam, quality's always supreme
Prices right, great selection, customer care tuned to perfection
(Product)'s network and tuna selection, (store) gets the best reception
(Product) offers a galaxy of quality and (store) are switched on to lower prices
(Promoter)'s TV, (product) for tea, another great (store)'s oppor-tuna-ty
Quality craftsmanship, style and precision, (product)'s range, the perfect decision
Quality's sky high, super selection, (store) gets a great reception
Rental charges not applying means much more (product)'s tuna buying
Sky's' the limit ! Great selection, 'dishing up' shopping perfection
(Store)'s 'astra' nomical for family shopping, no need for 'channel' hopping
(Store)'s discounts, beyond perception, are well received without exception
(Store)'s prices make me richer, (product)'s taste complete the picture
(Store)'s prices, without exception, always receive a great reception
(Store), (product), what a mixture, value, quality, get the picture !
Switch to (product) and you're tuned in for life
Their mission is to boldy go lower than any price has gone before
Their reputation's widely trusted, never needs to be adjusted
Their 'squeeze-able ' prices receive a good 'reception'
They 'dish' up heavenly quality at dependably earthly prices
They dish up a galaxy of selection

FOOD - BAKERY

Bread, biscuits, home baking, etc

All things light and beautiful, (product) bakes them all

Beautiful baking, fabulous fry, flexible (product), an excellent buy

Better baking finer fry is purely due to an excellent buy

Delicious biscuits, tropical beach, (product) and (store) bring it all in reach

Easy to use, easy to clean, easily the best for great cuisine

Eaten buttered or with a topping, once started there is no stopping

Even a beginner can bake a winner

Favourite biscuit, chance of cash, super trip, let's have a bash !

For perfect baking, saving pence, (product) provides the excellence

Four great flavours, four star treat, for lower prices, impossible to beat

Fruit or plain, I wish to see from whence the ingredients came (travel)

Funtime, treats and friendly faces, (store) is really going places

Gear-ed up cooks, re-quest the best, (product) quickly ensures success

Half-baked prices, great for mums, feeding (product) sized tums

I only mix in the best circles

Improving my cookery skills a desire, which (product) always inspire

Light bake, great fry, (product) is an excellent buy

(Location) adventure very exotic, a dream come true for this (product) chocoholic

Love the chocolate, love the savings, (product) at (store) satisfy my cravings

Man cannot live by bread alone but (product) makes it worth a try

Mouth watering biscuits, favourite store, competitive prices, I'm back for more!

Natural goodness makes it the natural choice

Plain milk orange or fruit, keeps me going to finish the route

Prize winning biscuits lucky me, a (location) holiday for sixty two 'p'

(Product) at (store)'s price is a choc-o-holics paradise

(Product) at (store)'s prices are half baked

(Product) butters me up with its half baked prices

(Product) can be buttered but not bettered

(Product) is 'choc-full' of great prizes and (store)'s 'chock-a-block' with low prices

(Product) makes baking a pleasure with time left for leisure

(Product) to be specific, is a pleasure to bake and tastes terrific

(Product)'s biscuit, tastebud teasers, exclusive offers, pocket pleasers

(Product)'s bread provides the fuel and (store) provides the tool

(Product)'s grains of rye and wheat make it a special sandwich treat

(Product)'s natural grains make it the toast of the town

(Product)'s variety is the slice of life

Stir fry, crispy, pastry light, highest quality, pure delight

Super biscuits, super store, strike me lucky I won't ask for more

The bread that I like could win me a bike

The sun always rises in the yeast

Their finest quality is no myth, my cakes surpass even Delia Smith's !

There's a chocolate treat to savour with a (location)'s flavour

They're a major contribution to a healthy constitution

They're what you need for energy and speed (cycles)

Thick chocolate outer, crispy inner, prizes or not, I'm still a winner

Thick rich chocolate with scrumptious inners, (product) from (store), are certain winners

When it comes to the crunch, there's no better munch

Chapter Nine : Prizewinning Slogans

FOOD - DAIRY

Butter, spreads, cheese, etc

A delicious flavour, spreads with ease, blended by (product), guaranteed to please

All the creamy, meadow fresh goodness we love is in (product) !

Blended vegetable oil and cream, makes a flavour that's supreme

Blending dairy cream and vegetable oil, clever (product) knows how to spoil

By perfectly blending oil and cream, (promoter)'s experts make (product) supreme

Churned for spreading straight from cold, creamy smooth (product) has riches untold !

Cream and fine ingredients mix, creating a flavour smooth and rich

Creamiest (product) blends, field-fresh flavour natural goodness my family favour

Creamy (product), thickly spread, makes a banquet out of bread

Creamy yet healthy, above all unique, perfectly blended with (product)'s technique

Delicious (product) is the perfect blend, creamy taste and less to spend !

Deliciously creamy, spreads from cold, on (product) I am totally sold

Deliciously creamy, tasting just right, generously spread, love at first bite

Expertly blended with lashings of cream, makes baking a joy, spreads supreme !

Feeling healthy, looking great, (store) and (product) watch my weight

Finest ingredients, expertly blended, country fresh flavour, spreads simply splendid !

Flavour outstanding, sandwiches divine, (product) on the label, the pleasure is mine

Fresh and cream, deliciously light, (product)'s always a meal time delight

Fresh tasting (product) is a dream where natural oil helps dairy cream

Full of goodness through and through, it's wholesome, light, delicious too

Golden goodness is in every bite, smooth, creamy, sheer delight !

It complements crackers and betters bread with a popularity so widespread

It is mature enough for adults, mild enough for kids

It tastes sublime without a doubt, (product) from (store), perfection throughout

Its buttery flavour makes the most of jacket potatoes, pastry and toast !

It's delicious, nutritious, tastefully splendid, creamy, smooth, perfectly blended

It's golden as the summer sun, wholesome, tasty and second to none

My experience is that hard times are over

On biscuits, crackers, toast or bread, its creamy taste is way ahead

On crispy crackers, toast or bread, creamy (product)'s the smoothest spread

Pastry's perfect, bread's a treat, (product) is the spread elite

Perfectly blended, toast of the town, creamy taste on white or brown

(Product)'s standards never waver, tops for creaminess, tops for flavour

(Product)'s the most versatile spread, wonderful in pastry, delicious on bread

(Product)'s creamy quality blend suits the healthy eating trend

Rich and creamy beyond compare, straight from the fridge - extraordinaire !

Smooth creamy flavour, delicious to eat, standards never waver, a genuine treat

Smooth, creamy and churned to perfection, quality, flavour and healthy nutrition

Superb ingredients, expertly blended, delightfully taste, (product) is splendid !

Tastefully blended, the brand to trust, butties to pastry, simply a must

Tempting, tasty and delicious, easy to spread and really nutritious

That creamy flavour without a doubt, tops anything its rivals 'churn' out

This versatile spread, creamy tasty - great on bread and makes wonderful pastry

FOOD - FRUIT & VEG

Potatoes

A little simmer brings out the summer
As Anthony murmured at Cleo's lips, I must have some Egyptian chips
Beautiful fresh taste, edible skin, all for me, none for the bin
Cleopatra found they did please her - their delicious taste made Julius 'Caesar'
Family lunch or gourmet dinner, (store)'s Jerseys are a certain winner
For family meals or haute cuisine's, (store)'s (potato) reign supreme
Good things come in little packets, straight from heaven without their jackets
Hot from the hob with a buttery knob, they're just the job !
I opt for the spud that's 'Hoe, Sow' - Good !
Local greens from British soils, enjoy mixing with the Royal's
No humble spud can ever compare, with (product)'s regal fare
Nothing can soil their reputation
Perfect meals in every way, come with 'the darling spuds of May'
(Product)'s 'Royal Earth Force' tastefully satisfies the loyal army of (store)'s shoppers
Queen Maris' beheaded, King Edward gone but (potato)'s still number one
Tasty skins, fluffy inners, these super spuds make perfect dinners
There is nothing under the earth quite like them
These buried treasures from (location)'s shore are well worth trading chips for
They're succulent, absolutely delicious, and to crown it all, extremely nutritious
They make other spuds look like 'old chips on the block'
They meet my great ex- 'spud'- tations
They're a winning ticket in the eating lottery
This tasty (potato) is a stunner, one swallow does make a summer
Under the ancient Egyptian mud, lies a treasure of a spud

Apples, pears, grapes, etc

Crisp juicy, tasty, nutrition, (product)'s a great tradition
Delicious crisp from orchard to table quality's assured with the (product) label
Deliciously crisp, never picked in haste, (product) have impeccable taste
Deliciously fruity from vine to table, quality assured with the (product) label
Each is a red and green thirst-quenching machine
Each seedless grape grows out West, is juicy, sweet and sun-caressed
Flavoursome plump crisp and juicy every sized (product) is an English beauty
Hollywood hills from (Store)'s tills, would be the fruit of smaller bills (grapes)
I can't get enough of the stuff - D'you C?
It's sweet refreshing zingy bite, (store)'s quality at a price that's right
Juicy, sweet and full of vitamin C, for a healthy lifestyle (product) is the key
Juicy, tasty, full of zest, (product)'s fruit are the best !
Naturally perfect for every occasion, picnics lunches or family invasion
Nothing added, nothing removed, natures best can't be improved
So sweet and juicy, ready to eat, (product), the anytime treats
Straight from the sun to (store)'s door, tasty, juicy, who needs more
Taking time to reach their prime, (product) taste sublime
Taste-a-peel, instant meal, extra nice at (store)'s price
The cream of the crop brings out the 'peach' in me
The pride of Nell Gwynn lies within
The (store)'s selection are grown to perfection
The sunshine flavour is a delight to savour
They get me off to a fresh start
Variety and quality, the best money can buy, delicious, the apple of my eye

Chapter Nine : Prizewinning Slogans

FOOD - MEAT

Beef, lamb, pork, etc

A tender cut of saddle back's the 'porkfect' aphrodisiac
Aga or wok, no price shock, two veg or cream, quality supreme
All strings right and beautiful suit eaters great and small
British breakfast is a great event, (product)'s bacon is money well spent
Breakfast time, sandwiches or evening meal, (product)'s bacon gives special appeal
Carefully tended, lush (location)'s grass, (product)'s beef is first in its class
Cattle reared wild and free, guarantee quality, naturally
Crest on the label, guarantees best on the table
Delicious (store)'s British Pork even offers a taste of New York
Expert selection, matured to perfection, traditional criteria for beef that's superior
Family fiesta or romantic dinner British Pork's an all time winner
Family meal or party hosting, (store)'s beef gives others a roasting
For many mighty meaty reasons, they're the sausage for all seasons
From sty to fry it's a perfect buy
Having gone the whole hog, you bring home the bacon
I wouldn't give anything else a second butcher's
It's 'streaks' ahead of the rest
It's my favourite bacon, reasonably priced, nutritious, delicious already sliced
It's tasty, nutritious, perfectly cured, favours enhanced and quality assured
It can cook in ovens or woks, bless it's little cotton hocks
It deserves an oinkore
It gets joint honours for its degree of reliability and flexibility
It knocks the stuffing out of the opposition
It's easy to cook, lovely and lean, perfect choice for British cuisine
It's produced from pigs reared in the pink, keeping us perky
It's the 'pork' of the town from a store of renown
It's the beef in its prime, traditionally matured to taste divine
It's the best in its niche and sealed with a quiche
It's gammonteed to put a smile on your chops
Makes frying less trying
Matured on the bone, prime selection, whatever the cut, beef perfection
Once fried, never forgotten
Oven, grill or pan, it is perfectly matured for feeding my clan
Sizzling breakfast, gourmet dinner, tasty lunch, I'm on a winner
Specially selected, traditionally matured, (store)'s beef's flavour's assured
Sunshine, spice everything nice, that's what these pigs are made of
Taste of (product), superbly presented, leaves palates pleased and pockets contented
Tender beef, perfectly coloured, delicious, nutritious and easily afforded
Tenderest rashers, 'backed' by great reputation, 'streaks' ahead of the rest, a sizzling sensation
The sizzle siz it all
There is no miss-steak wheel meat again
They only select the best and don't 'mull' over the rest
To buy other pork would be cupid
Unbeatable value, lean and nutritious, a firm favourite, looking delicious
When you're on an economy drive you get more miles per gammon
With your 'pause' on perfect porkies, there will be many repeats!
You can roast it, or grill it, even stuff it or fillet
Your confidence in (store) is never shaken especially when buying (product)'s bacon

LAUNDRY

Washing powders, conditioners, etc

A love of material things is deeply ingrained in it

Awash with economy and efficiency, (product) cleaning with 'dazzling' proficiency

At only 40 cool degrees, (product) shifts the grease with utmost ease

Awash with great qualities, this outstanding pair, clean up on consumer care

Being powerful yet kind, they take loads off my mind

Both 'duet' with expertise, shopping's a pleasure, drying's a breeze

Both give freshness and value and leave me ex-static

Both take pride in the freshness inside

Breath of spring softly blows, pleasing my pocket and my clothes

Brilliant performance, sensible bills, efficient at last with (product) skills

By counteracting winter rain, this super prize will keep me sane

Capturing beautiful scents and saving valuable pence, definitely makes economical sense

Chocolate casserole and chilli sauce are blasted away with equal force

Chosen first to last, its awash with quality unsurpassed

Cleaner cuffs, fresher socks, without those dreaded checkout shocks

Clothes are fresh as mountain breezes and (store)'s prices always pleases

Come hail, rain, sleet, snow, through my washing summer breezes blow

Crinkles vanish, so does static, no more ironing, I'm ex-static

Dry fresh laundry, incredibly inventive, (product) from (store) gives more incentive

Easy to use, fresh every time, smells like the country, simply divine

Economy, speed and a wash that's bright, (product) definitely got it right

Faced with such a might foe, stubborn stains give up and go

Every spring and summer sheet, makes clothes smell fresh and meadow sweet

Every wash day wet or fine, outdoor freshness would be fine

For lightness and brightness, it takes a lot to improve this whiteness

Forget the lottery, this'll do fine to guarantee a winning line

Fragrantly fresh with softness abundant, this fabulous pair makes clothes lines redundant

Having plenty of clout, there are no problems to be ironed out

I want the cleanest possible wash at the lowest possible costs

I'm under no illusion, this is the washday blues solution

In the wise 'buy' election, it's the greatest soap selection

It ensures quality in the fabric of our lives

It is macro powered detergent for micro cost

It makes an impression without leaving a mark

It's a cool operator in a dirty world

It's an automatic winner, for this newly wed beginner

It's programmed to be the leading soap

It's programmed to clean, while designed to be green

Power and gentle action combine to lighten and whiten my load

(Product)'s travelled to a new dimension in futuristic stain prevention

(Store)'s prices won't clean out your pockets but (product)'s excellence will

The answer my friend is glowing in the wind

The cost to wash would be nominal, but results would be phenomenal

The price pegging means value on every line

They brighten washing with lesser expense, a package like this makes common sense

This home banker gives the best results to get a winning line

Whatever the challenge whatever the grime, sparkling clean every time

Chapter Nine : Prizewinning Slogans

MOTORING

Car, petrol, accessories, etc

A car you can trust is a family must

A contented car load makes light of the longest road

A top performer that second to none, like (product), my number one

Car of the future, awash with technology, a real break through in driving ecology

(Car)'s door now a-jar, (store) and (product) unsur-pasta-ble by far

(Car)'s hot wheels get clean away

Classy appliances, brand new wheels, (product) 'drive' the greatest deals

Convert to this gear, to be in fashion all year

Corsa I'm highly motor-vated, by the spreads they've created

Day or night, whatever the hour, turn the key, release the power

Driving authenticity home, (product)'s car-is-ma pasta-port to Rome

Elegant, eye catching, effortless style, (product) and (car) so versatile

Excellent quality is certified, high performance verified, motorists everywhere satisfied

Family key words, taste and nutrition, quickly (product) add ignition

Favourite characters, pasta test, its formula 'won' on tomatoness

For appearance, classic style, you'll attract attention all the while

For quality, style and priceless care, you can 'relion' this ultimate pair

From bumper to bumper, beginning to end, the (car) is the family's friend

From motorway melee to city crawl, designed for tomorrow, protects overall

Great sounds amid quiet luxury product a transport of delight

I'd have a clutch of manifold advantages from a great distributor

I look clean, smell fresh with (car) I'm bound to impress

Impeccably fitted, exciting to run, elegance and chic, second to none

In a world beyond my imagination (product) still lead in lubrication

It circulates with ease giving performance to please

It's better by miles, a premier solution to coupon pollution

Its matchless performance, quality and style, carries you spellbound mile after mile

Ma-car-oni what an exciting twist to (product)'s deliciously re-sauce-ful list

Motoring perfection on the move, (product) when the going gets smooth

Motorway miles or city crawl, designed for the 90's protects all

Own car stolen, what a crisis, new one needed, (car)'s nicest

(Product) is a formula one cannot surpass

(Product)'s protection, (store)'s care, (car) on road, romance in air

(Product) and (car) inspires motor-vation of tasteful desire

(Product) can breathe new life into expiring engines

Repairs, accidents, makes good as new, take the chequered flag as the number one glue

Skirts and sweaters in cahoots are joined by bonnets, sometimes boots

(Store)'s shoppers seek exquisite style, (car) supply it mile and mile

Superb performance, designed with style, my future's bright, mile after mile

The (car) cruises trouble free, while (store) pampers the family

The ultimate in style and flair, they suit the occasions anywhere

They both share exceptional elegance with fantastic performance

They provide power through gears and pleasure to the ears

Unbeatable quality, eye-catching style, travel triumphantly mile after mile

With precision and style that's hard to beat, (product) puts me in the driving seat

SPORT

Cycling

Avoid motorway melee, city crawl, ideal for families and fun for all
Cycling renews that youthful thrill, for this wrinkly who's over the hill
Enjoy endless days of leisure, on the bike that's built for pleasure
They're wheelie great to keep us active, family agrees (promoter)'s bikes are attractive

Football

A regular crowd puller, there's no other lager with a flavour that's fuller
Brewed to full flavour in (product)'s tradition, my favourite lager's in premier position
Every (product) turns out fine, without the need for extra time
For every goal, save, smile and tear, (product)'s quality is strikingly clear
Sparkling performance, striking display, spectacular result, match of the day
There's no substitute for delicious (product), it's the permanent fixture on any table

Golf

Driver, iron, putter or wedge, (product) has the edge
Great (product), super store, 'putt' together who needs more
Playing 'a round' with (golfer), followed by a game of golf !!
What I lose on the rounds, I gain on the swings

Horse Racing

As they always stay fresh 'furlong' these well packed favourites finish strong
Quicker fresher, satisfaction immense, no wonder others fall at the first fence
Winning horse needs top jockey winning picnic needs top coffee

Motor Racing

A brilliant finish from a fine performer, superior on straights and corners
Ahead on quality it's tradition, puts (product) in pole position
Amongst a multitude of tins, this roaring success always wins
Brushing aside other tins, (product)'s finish always wins

Olympic Events

Olympic games and eastern delight, this cocktail sounds just right
Olympic sensations, standing ovation, paradise location, what an equation
Top performance, second to none, (product) in (location) show how its done

Skiing

There's snow risk of (product) ever going downhill
To 'summit' all up their range is the top
United we stand, united we'll fall, bruises soon fade, it's the fun we'll recall
When I'm 'on the piste' I insist on 'off-peak' prices

Snooker

Without (product) you're snookered
You can focus in and pocket great gifts

Tennis

From grass to clay, (product) captures the play
(Product) serve aces, bring smiles to our faces
(Product) never lets the grass grow under your feet
Technological experts have conceded, (product) remain top seeded

Chapter Nine : Prizewinning Slogans

TRAVEL - COUNTRIES

Africa and the Middle East

Cleopatra found they did please her - their delicious taste made Julius 'Caesar'
They leave my family 'asping' for more
To weigh anchor in Casablanca then have a fez of the heart
Up the Amazon, down the Nile, service is wider than crocodiles' smiles

Asia and the Far East

Authentic tasting (product) in a wok, says hello India, Japan and Bangkok
Midas touches my Yen to roam, securing sterling far from home
(Product)'s oriental saucery tricks make delectable dishes disappear quick
Refreshing accompaniment for hot vindaloo; cooler than cucumber, tastier too !

Australia

Hasta la vista, Manchester rain, aloha Hawaii, Sydney and Maine
I'd go to Bondi Beach, because whenever I open a deck chair it's upside-down
Sydney harbours it crate after crate, Alice Springs for the exciting bait

Europe - France

A touch of (product) enhances gourmet cuisine, would love some French ambience to set the scene
Boutiques and bistros, Le Metro, Montmatre, like (product), it's captured my heart!
Brié, French wine and a baguette, is the nearest to heaven I'll ever get
Channel hopping, Christmas shopping would be magnifiqué, so I've 'mustard' up my hopes and I'm free next week !
Delicious mushroom, tasty cheese, my family parlez'more mum, please

Don't leave things to pure bonné chancé, the (product) can guide you en vacancé
Eiffel in love with delight at the end of the tunnel
I'd ferry across there, merci !
I'd get plastered in Paris !
It's the perfect spot for a spending spree, a bit like springtime in Pareé !
Legions of travellers agree, its the civilised way to cross the sea
Shuttle's swiftness, French cuisine, (product)'s guidance, my dream team
The Arc, the Elyseés, the Eiffel above, where better to make a proposal of love
They offer such quality at prices so fair, I haven't Degaulle to shop elsewhere!
Yen for travelling, mark my word, cheque-ing out others is franc-ly absurd
While cruising the Seine, sipping champagne, I could fall for my wife all over again

Europe - Germany

Breathtaking scenery seen by car, like my (store), Germany would be wunderbar
Consistent quality, every bottle I buy in German or French style, sweet, crisp or dry
For 'Sterling' value, it's full 'Marks'
Having selected the finest German wine, (store) will ensure a wonderful time
Lunch al fresco, wurst with rye, tastes wunderbar with (product)'s dry
Luxurious flavour quality that's rare, bouquets rivalling sweetest Rhine air
Oompah music, steins of bier, bratwurst, strudel and festive cheer
(Product)'s obviously best, at this Bavarian Oktoberfest
The best in my Stein, the pleasure's all mein
This picturesque home of fairytale saga, offers delightful wines, food and lager
This wine from the Rhine is perfect every time

TRAVEL - COUNTRIES

Europe - Italy

Bistecca alla florentina, moonlight and a signorina

I can-a-letto myself choose without going pasta my limit

It has the vision of Rome, the passion of Naples and the Inspiration of Venice

It's my pasta-port to Italian delight, conveniently located, priced just right!

Italian food just like in Rome, only a (store) ride from home

Pocket the pennies for Italian break, spaghetti, vino and a pizza cake

Rome and Venice come one step nearer, (product)'s goods worth every Lira

(Store)'s shopping is a cinch, I go Italian without feeling the pinch !

To explore in depth, this lovely nation, they're the 'numero uno' combination

Touch of Italy, my cooking flair, (product) and (store), a perfect pair

Veneto sausage and Italian bread, complement (product)'s softest red

With a family to impress, (product) 'cannelloni' be a success

With inside knowledge and helpful tips, they're the ultimate experts in Italian trips

North America - Canada

Any other (product) would make me grizzly, unbearable and pine !

Canada Affords Natural and Delightful Attractions

Every 'pitcher' tells a story, Canadians love (product)'s glory

First rate taste, spruce presentation, is their 'province' and 'dominion'

I'd see Buffalo, without the Bill !

Its refreshing power lifts me up higher than the CN tower

(Product)'s ring pulls, like Niagara Falls, are my favourite watering holes

North America
United States of America

After stylish Fifth Avenue - top for the shops, tantalising (product) is 'top of the pops'

American taste, American dream, (product) and (store) are my dream team

Anywhere else 'Ill'inois it's true, only (store) 'scores' with such premium brew

Chicago Bulls, 'thirst' class team, price and beer that is supreme !

Cinnamon swirls, raisins plump and fruity, given (product) more body than a Baywatch beauty

Deliciously fruity from vine to table, quality assured with the California label

Deliciously mild, full of taste, (product) Unites the States

Glasses are raised, cheers, bottoms up, stateside style they balance the bucks

It's the (store) way to have a nice day

LA sunshine, nightime raver, Xmas early for this (store)'s saver

My postcard would read, `Florida great, weather fine, thank you (promoter) for a smashing time'

Nickels, dollars, pounds or pence, (product) at (store) makes good cents

(Product), the American cheerleader

(Product) the beer, basketball the sport, (store) makes Chicago my thirst resort

Skiing delights me, Colorado excites me, hope (promoter) invites me

Sweet and juicy, California's pride, hours of sunshine sealed inside

Their Minnie prices galore, take the Mickey out of every other store

Together they're a winning team, a passport to my American dream

We'd travel the state with our (product) beside us, and relax in the style that (promoter) provide us

When the USA is just a ring pull away !

With warming sun and gentle breeze, California (product)'s are picked to please

CHAPTER TEN

Lynspiration

When I launched *Intacomps* newsletter in June 1994, my aim was to provide a practical and useful service to compers, both beginners and constant winners. After speaking to many compers, the majority want information as to where they can find entry forms to current competitions, lists of previous winning tiebreakers for inspiration, details of new publications and general chitchat on changing events on the comping scene.

Nothing is more frustrating than making a special effort to go into town to track down entry forms, to find you come home several hours later, with weary feet and no forms. With *Intacomps*, produced quarterly in March, June, September and December, the next time you go entry form hunting, you need only take a list of which stores have comps, thus saving time.

There are many Instant Win type competitions currently on the go. You will not find many of these mentioned in *Intacomps* as your chances of a winning prize is based on pure luck and are less than for those contests requiring skill.

Intacomps prides itself on mentioning some of the more unusual competitions around. After all, you may visit your local supermarket on a daily or weekly basis, thus collecting any entry forms as and when they appear. You are less likely to make weekly visits to garden centres, banks and building societies other than your own, petrol stations other than your usual one, or large out-of-town shopping malls. When you see a specific competition of interest you can then make a special journey to locate the form.

In addition to my own entry form safaris, *Intacomps* keeps you up-to-date with competition details, by receiving forms from five entry form services, mentioned below.

Entry Forms at Your Service !

Some readers do live in rather remote areas of the country, where access to nearby towns and cities is limited, therefore the number of entry forms found is very low. Even though your attention has been alerted to a particular comp, you may not be able to obtain a form yourself.

Should this be the case, you may like to consider subscribing to one or more of these services, some of whom give a personal service in that they try to accommodate their subscriber's wishes as to types of forms. Subscribers are then sent a pack of different entry forms each month. Some stores only target certain branches for particular competitions and it is possible therefore to obtain entry forms which your local branch do not have.

The following are a selection with addresses, should you wish to write enclosing a stamped addressed envelope please, for further details:

Walton's Mountain

Chris and Don Walton are keen and enthusiastic compers, having won many prizes, including holidays abroad and a Rover car. Even though they have access to a wide range of stores in Essex, they travel several times a week into London, to search for more elusive forms. They issue a newsletter a few times a year, to keep subscribers up to date with events.

>   Walton's Mountain
>   195 Rutland Road
>   Chelmsford
>   Essex CM1 4BW

Formwork

Formwork is probably the longest established entry form service. Launched in 1979, specialising in individual requirements based on an efficient checklist system. Requests, needs, preferences are noted, ensuring that forms are regularly reserved for subscribers. News updates with answers, advice on magazine, plain paper and on-pack contests included.

>   Formwork
>   PO Box 67
>   Bishops Stortford
>   Herts CM23 3NN

Anne Lawton

Anne has been supplying entry forms for several years now and offers a varied selection of both supermarket and non-supermarket forms.

>   Anne Lawton
>   113 Sprinkbank Road
>   Chell Heath, Stoke on Trent ST6 4HL

Teldata

Teldata has been supplying entry forms for six years, with a free swap shop available to subscribers. Monthly packs contain up to thirty forms while 'Top 10 Packs', made up of ten of the best current forms are available for those with less time on their hands.

>   Teldata
>   5 Well Walk
>   The Knap
>   Barry, South Glamorgan CF62 6SU

Chapter Ten : Lynspiration

Anne Robertson

Anne, an enthusiastic comper for sixteen years, has been supplying entry forms since 1994. Along with husband Robert, they regularly visit large shopping centres in Scotland to search for forms. Subscribers specific requests are noted and they do their best to comply.

> Anne Robertson
> 141 Sandpiper Place
> Greenhills
> East Kilbride, Lanarkshire G75 8UP

Intacomps Update Service

As new forms arrive at our offices several times a week, the time lapse between quarterly issues of *Intacomps*, means you may miss details of competitions which close in the interim period. To keep readers up-to-date, a monthly Current Competition and Free-To-Enter Update is available for the interim months of January, February, April, May, July, August, October and November. This service is exclusively for *Intacomps* subscribers. The only charge made is a first class stamp to cover printing costs and a stamped addressed envelope.

Other features in the *Intacomps* newsletter are free-to-enter and magazine competitions. You can find out which magazines are available free of charge and how to get your name on relevant mailing lists to receive details of future promotions, offers and competitions.

To help you with research, the Facts Not Fiction page gives such details of who won the latest golfing tournament, snooker championship, new world record holders etc. After all, reference books are only as up to date as the time they go to print, and keen compers like to keep abreast of the news, for answering possible future competition questions.

To provide ideas and inspiration for writing your own tiebreakers, there is an ongoing Compers Course, Simply Slogans tiebreakers and Words Of Phrase, which gives tiebreaker ideas on one specific product or theme.

Intacomps also reviews comping services which may be of interest to you. There is reader involvement too with letters, articles, snippets of information and in-house competitions to enter. Here, from previous copies of *Intacomps* is a delightful article from Jill Dick, the winner of our Readers Article Competition, and an apt and entertaining story from Tony Crafter.

Priceless China by Jill Dick

My prize in the department store's anniversary draw was a complete bone china dinner set for six people and I was excited when I was greeted by the Manager on the morning of the presentation. The poor man had a streaming cold and looked as if the sooner the day was over the happier he would be, but he was obviously determined to do his best and quickly led me to the store's china department where the event was to be held. On a raised platform in the centre of the floor area was a table with a full range of expensive dishes perfectly arranged on a white linen tablecloth.

Between sneezes the Manager introduced me to a handful of men representing the promoters and waved his hand over the beautiful tableware. "We'll deliver it all to you afterwards," he snuffled, pushing his hanky in his pocket. "We don't want any breakages, do we?"

Then he dashed off to round up some assistants so a rather disinterested press photographer could give the store good publicity in the local paper.

After some hesitation about who should stand where and whether the prize or the prizewinner should take centre stage, the Manager took his place behind the table, blew his nose loudly and at the word "Right?" we all gave our camera-ready smiles. The photographer clicked and everyone relaxed.

"Thank..." began the Manager. With a tremendous crash all the valuable china landed in a heap on the floor.

There were horrified shrieks before the store assistants rallied round trying to pick up the pieces and jolly along shoppers attracted by the noise while the Manager sank into speechless misery. One of the promoters took me on one side, muttered that I would still receive the prize as promised - unbroken - and I was swiftly ushered away.

"What had happened? Did the table collapse? Had someone let off a bomb?

I scanned the next edition of the local paper. There was no mention of me, the store, the presentation or the disaster - and I realised I might be the only person (until now) who would for all time share the Manager's dreadful secret.

He had inadvertently stuffed the corner of the tablecloth in his pocket with his hanky and when he moved away from the table, the cloth - and everything on it - went with him.

oooooOOOooooo

Saturday Morning Pictures by Tony Crafter

"Why the hell don't they number these pages !" cursed *Harry Johnson. He had been flicking impatiently through the advertisements in the Saturday magazine, looking for the crossword on page 48. By the time he found it, he had lost interest, having been overcome by an irresistible urge to savour one of Worth's delicious broccoli flans. Jane, his wife, was already out shopping. "Damn !" he cursed again, "I should have asked her to get some".

Chapter Ten : Lynspiration

Sighing, he pulled on his coat, not even stopping to consider that he had just eaten a hearty breakfast. What's more, he detested broccoli.

When he arrived at the supermarket, Harry wasted no time in asking an assistant for directions to the flan and quiche section. "End of the aisle on your right sir, " she replied, "just follow the crowds." "Thank you, but they must be Worth's", asserted Harry "If they're not Worth's, they're not worth eating !"

If they're not Worth's they're not worth eating !

Then he scuttled off with his trolley, leaving the assistant scratching his head and muttering, "That's what they all said.'

Harry had to fight against a tide of flan-laden trolleys, all being pushed by smiling shoppers declaring that anything other than Worth's just wasn't worth eating.

When he reached the required section, there were rows of empty shelves and a little old lady was reaching up hopefully towards the top of these. "Could you help me please, young man?" she pleaded. "Not likely !" said Harry as he scooped them into his trolley and sprinted off towards the check-out.

***

"But you hate broccoli" reasoned Jane, as Harry crouched in front of the freezer, trying to find space for a dozen flans. "Yes, I know, but they are Worth's and anything else is just not worth eating", he said, as though trying to educate the unenlightened. "Pardon?" Jane blinked in disbelief. "I said, if they're not Worth's... Gee I hate broccoli, why have I bought all these flans ?"

The following Saturday, Harry returned with 25 boxes of Figgins Firelighters because, he explained, "they save second lightings and lighting seconds". Jane explained that they had the fireplace bricked in five years ago. "Never mind!" he retorted, they could always enjoy the ample supplies of Sampan Stir Fries.

"Why have you brought enough to feed the entire Terracota Army?" queried Jane. "Because", he grinned - "Eastern flavours I unlock, by being wicked with my wok!" "You wouldn't know a wok from a walking stick !" she screamed, "What is the matter with you, Harry ?" "I don't know," he said sheepishly.

When Harry returned from shopping the following Saturday with 20 tubs of Angelface Skin Cream, Jane didn't even ask why he'd bought them, but made an immediate appointment to see their GP.

"I think Harry's going mad", she explained to the kindly old family Doctor "Why do you say that, my dear ?", he asked gently. "Well, he keeps making strange shopping expeditions. Today he came home with 20 tubs of facial cream." "Hm...it wasn't Angelface, was it?' "Yes!" she cried, "how did you know?"

"Because, my dear, 'The years of care behind Angelface put the cares of the years behind you'. Tell me, did he manage to buy any Simpson's One-Size Surgical Stockings - 'Thick or thin, long or short, they give your legs their firm support'. I managed to snap up a family pack at Lamb's Stores because 'Those who flock there won't get fleeced !' .... Mrs Johnson, where are you going?"

When Jane arrived home, she didn't bat an eyelid at the ocean of Hyacinth Toilet Rolls spread out across the hallway. "Harry, we've got to talk !" she called out.

He appeared from the living room and looked bashfully at the toilet rolls. "Can't afford orchids", he recited, "so I treat myself to Hyacinths in loo!" "Harry", she said gently, "we've got to talk."

***

"It's the same every Saturday", he pleaded, "I've always done the magazine crossword, but I can't any more. Before I get to page 48, I have to dash off to buy something. It's like incontinence of the wallet !" He was starting to look haunted.

"Maybe you're spending too long reading the advertisements," suggested Jane. "No, I don't even look at them. I just flick through the pages like this..." Jane watched over his shoulder. "Is that all you do? You definitely don't read them?" "No", he pleaded. "Strange", she said, "Ah, well, must dash - got some shopping to do. See you later". "But Jane, how about my prob..." Too late, she'd gone.

Harry sat down and looked blankly at the magazine. The answer had to lie within its pages. He slowly turned each one, reading the advertisements carefully. Nothing unusual so far, just the same old uninspiring platitudes for unremarkable products. When he reached the back page, he started at the front and went through again. That was when he noticed the coloured dots. Nothing unusual in itself, but these were grouped in an apparently random cluster, about the size of a pack of book matches at the bottom of some of the pages. As he was trying to figure out their significance, his teenage son came in and casually looked over his shoulder.

"Autostereograms, Dad," he remarked idly. "What have record players go to do with anything?" asked Harry. "No, autostereograms" laughed the boy, "a series of overlapping dots created by a computer programme. Concentrate on them long enough and a three-dimensional image will emerge from the chaos. Sometimes it takes hours, or even days, to see the image, but when you do, the effect is amazing. They're all the rage in Japan and America." After his son had left the room, Harry continued staring at the dots until he was cross-eyed and blue in the face, but they remained a confused cluster of meaningless shapes.

Two hours later, he heard Jane's car pulling into the drive and, as his concentration relaxed, so the image appeared in tiny but startling clarity. It was a three-dimensional cereal box, bearing the message. 'A bowl of crunchy Wheaty Shred would Rip Van Winkle out of bed ! Buy some now.'

Harry gasped at the sheer genius of it. "This is subliminal advertising raised to new dimensions!" he said to himself. "The eye doesn't always see the message, but the brain does ! The pages deliberately aren't numbered so you have to flick through them to get to the one you want. As you do so, the command to buy the product is catapulted into your subconscious. Brilliant!" Harry leapt to his feet as Jane entered the room. "I've got it !" he cried.

"You've got it !" she laughed excitedly, "So have I. A real find. I had to fight hard but guess what I got ? The last ten boxes of Wheaty Shred on the shelf !"

* All characters fictitious

ooooOOOoooo

At Your Service

It is lovely to receive readers articles and letters, and any constructive comments or ideas are taken seriously. Indeed, the updates and introduction of readers' articles came from readers suggestions. Following an *Intacomps* survey, in which compers said they'd like more free-to-enter comps, this lead to the publication of a monthly A5 booklet, *Free-For-All*.

Ideas from entering my own competitions and suggestions from readers led to the launch of three series of booklets, namely, *Prizewinning Slogans*, *Intaslogans* and *Info-finder*.

Prizewinning Slogans, with their tiebreakers, are published every six months in March and September, to keep you up-to-date.

As you look through these tiebreakers, you not only gain inspiration for writing your own compilations but have an edge on the 'competition' by noting the styles certain promoters and handling houses favour. For example, two years ago, the winner of a seed company's competition penned:

   (Product) supply what others lack, quality seeds in every pack

This slogan simply states what the product supplies and gives praise. Interestingly, the winner of the following year's competition used a similar style of slogan with:

   (Product) grew to fame by putting quality behind their name

Now this is not to say because this style was chosen twice, all future ones will follow the same style, but I've found it serves as a useful guideline.

You may find it helpful to browse through lists of winning tiebreakers for a specific promoter. You may then note the majority of the tiebreakers contain a play on words, therefore, should you submit a tiebreaker with a play on words, you are likely to have a much better chance of success. You may also decide, should multiple entries be allowed, to send in a completely different style as well. After all we cannot possibly know what the judges are looking for, but it does provide a starting point from which to pen your own entries.

The *Intaslogans* series of handy size booklets enables you to select one booklet for a specific product or theme. You may be writing an entry for washing powder, which offers washing machine prizes. *Intaslogans : Laundry* inspires you with tiebreakers, not only for washing powder, but for fabric conditioners, tumble drying products and washing machines. The booklet also contains a few words and phrases which you may find useful when perfecting your tiebreakers.

Some compers find writing tiebreakers so time consuming, they have little time for researching the first part of the tasks. To help towards solving this problem the unique *Info-Finder* series was launched. Categorised in products or themes, this is similar to *Intaslogans* but has the additional facility of providing factual information. A real bonus should you find access to a library limited, or shortage of time.

The first booklet in the *Info-Finder* series, *Info-Finder : Travel - North America*, has factual information on the United States of America, Canada and Mexico. It provides information on Presidents, States, Space flights and the Disney theme, together with relevant words, phrases and tiebreakers for inspiration. Here is an extract on California:

Info-finder : Travel - North America
United States of America - California

Capital - Sacramento
California is known as the Golden State and is the third largest. It joined the Union on 9 September 1850, as the 31st State. It's name is derived from an imaginary island featured in a Spanish romance. The Colorado River forms the southern portion of the Eastern border. Also in the East is the Sierra Nevada Mountains which has Mount Whitney approx. 14,494 feet (4418m). Hollywood is a district in Los Angeles and associated as the centre of the motion picture industry, the first movie studio being established in 1911. Los Angeles is home to the original Disneyland Park. The Golden Gate suspension bridge spans the Golden Gate Strait which is at the entrance to San Francisco Bay and separates this from the Pacific Ocean. Building commenced in 1933 with completion in 1937. Its length is 4200 feet (1280m). Largest city - Los Angeles.

Tiebreakers

American fruits plus Californian sun, equals unique taste and star-spangled fun
Bronx to California 'cut' for 'action' product 'star' and give 'premier' satisfaction
California's Appealing Luscious Intoxicating Flavours of Real Note from Nearby stores
Californian sun grows fruit so fine, they produce the most superior wine
Californian wine so tasty and fine is delicious, desirable and divine
Charming And Lively, Invariably Fruity Or Robust, Nicely Inexpensive, Absolute Nectar
Deliciously fruity from vine to table, quality assured with the Californian label
Drinking the golden valley sunshine of California

Chapter Ten : Lynspiration

> Each seedless grape grows 'out West' is juicy, sweet and sun-caressed
> From simple meals to festive treats, Californian wines cannot be beat
> Hollywood Hills from store's tills, would be the fruit of smaller bills
> Hollywood, Disneyland, Frisco, LA, these dreams and product make Mothers Day
> It makes me feel great in this Californian State
> It puts you in the Sunshine State
> It tastes fresh and fruity, oozing sunshine and California's beauty
> It's Charming, Aromatic, Light, Innovative, Fruity, Original, Refreshing Nectar, Inexpensive and News
> Low in Calories affordable and nutritious, a tempting treat, succulent and delicious
> Passports neglected, photos a hoot, we'd thrill jetting on (product)'s sunshine route
> (Product)'s box of delights, might transport me to Californian sights

In addition to the enjoyment and challenge of entering competitions, it's lovely to enjoy the relaxing and social side of our hobby, which includes writing to pen pals and meeting other compers. Similarly, whilst I publish booklets which will be useful and inspirational, it is also pleasant to be able to read light-hearted articles and other interesting snippets of comping trivia. It seems an opportune time, therefore, to mention Winn Sommor's delightful booklet, published annually each Spring. The following is a review which appeared in *Intacomps*.

Winn's Comp-Elation by Lynne Suzanne
March 1995 - Intacomps

A few years ago, Winn and I met up at the Scarborough Comp Camp, when she introduced her first booklet - *Winn Some More*. I found it to be entertaining, but oh dear ! The questions she sets in those comps - leaves much to be desired.

Now those readers who are *Intacomps* subscribers or who read Winn's Lincolnshire *Target* newspaper features, will know we are the best of friends, but have a friendly 'rivalry' between us, in which I accuse her of setting the most awful brain teaser questions for her competitions.

Now to be fair, part of the challenge of comping is the satisfaction of completing the tasks, but with Winn's booklet, I found myself not only enjoying the challenge, but learning some new information along the way but was filled with a desire to 'complete these damn answers, if it kills me' Only joking, Winn! I sent off my entries and was quite optimistic of winning a prize, after all there were bound to be low entries with some of the questions she'd set. One thing we all learn as compers - is never underestimate the competition. Needless to say I didn't win a prize!

I was delighted when Winn brought out her second booklet, aptly entitled *Winn Some More Again,* or perhaps it should have been: 'Oh No! Not Winn Sommor Again!' We are the best of friends, honestly ! Surprisingly enough, some of the questions had actually got easier, but the booklet was still full of amusing anecdotes, articles, a variety of competitions and jolly good value for money. I persevered, but no, didn't win again !

Do you believe in third time lucky ? Well, if so, here is my chance to try again, because Winn is bringing out her third booklet in April, entitled *Winn's Comp-Elation*. Intrigued to find out why she'd opted for a different title and to ask her about this latest venture, I popped along to Boston to have a chat and find out what goes on behind the scenes.

I asked Winn if she could tell us about the competition tasks she set and how these are judged. Obviously, entrants have a much better chance of winning prizes in Winn's booklets as she limits the number which are sent out, each one being given a security coded number which entrants must submit with their entries.

When asked about the judging, Winn told me a few surprising facts and results to some of the competitions she had set in her last booklet. The competition to win £20 book token posed questions about books and authors and created no problems for entrants, except question five, which asked 'What is the common link between the names Isaac Bickerstaff, T Fribble and Lemuel Gulliver.' The correct answer was these are all pseudonyms of Jonathon Swift. Everyone who made the connection with the author was considered correct. The tedious task of checking was made pleasurable by one lady's answer 'None of them wrote *Thomas the Tank Engine*.' I know exactly how she feels! All Winn could answer to this was 'She obviously has the same whacky sense of humour as me.' Enough said !

The teatime quiz to win a cordless kettle had very straightforward factual questions, or were they? One question posed:' A Chinook, karaburan, khamsin, buran and gragale are all types of what?' All entrants except for two correctly stated winds, the other two said helicopters - surely not? At this stage, Winn says she did not reject the entries but prayed hard that the first drawn would state winds and the odds were in her favour. She adds with a laugh, 'I may be well know for setting tough questions, but I also make sure I am totally fair and am prepared to make thorough checks if I receive answers I did not expect.'

With tiebreaker tasks there are no right or wrong answers for Winn to worry about and she says it is all down to the personal choice of the judges. Entrants had been asked to complete the tiebreaker 'I did not know I was suffering from Comperitus until ...' in no more than twleve apt, original and amusing words. Winn was happy with the judges' choice as it had been on her own short list of six favourites:

> When bedtime came, my little lad said, read me another slogan, dad

It may interest you to know very few entrants made any real attempt to be amusing and this had to be taken into consideration when judging. The winner received a useful comping package.

Although Winn's booklet contained 28 A4 pages with a total of fifteen separate competitions, the final comp she wanted to tell us about proved to be the most popular. This was to come up with a suitable title for her next booklet, using up to eight apt and original words. Many entrants thought along the same lines and so were eliminated. As this booklet will be her third, many people had used the word 'tri' in the title, turning the idea into double meaning such as 'Try Sommor To Win'. There were many versions of 'The Winn-ing Post' and Winn Sommor's Encore. The words Hat-trick and Treble were frequently used and

Chapter Ten : Lynspiration

'You've Got To Be In To Winn' theme was also evident plus three identical 'Third Time Lucky' titles. The short listed titles were:

    A Little Feminine Wintuition
    Worthy Winners Win Within
    Sommor To Winn
    Bound To Win (note the play on words)
    Winns'head Revisited

When she came to choose the winner however, she took into consideration her booklets don't just contain prize competitions but articles, true comping stories, poetry, information and special comping services and offers. The prize of a bottle of whisky and a book were awarded to a lady, who had used a clever double meaning, short, original and very apt title, so Winn will be proud to call her next booklet:

    Winn's Comp-Elation

Winn's booklets are launched annually in April and further details can be obtained from:

    Winn Sommor
    Erica Handling House
    Dept 47, Tattershall
    Lincoln, LN4 4NR

oooOOOooo

Following that article, Winn's comps have now been judged. I know you're just dying to know if I've won a prize, aren't you ? Er... well, er... NO ! I have to admit defeat, yet again. Still, there's always her next booklet to look forward to.

After chatting to Winn about her booklet, we swapped amusing anecdotes. It was then we decided, 'why not produce a comping booklet together'. A book of all the amusing incidents which have happened to us and other compers. So if you've any snippets, anecdotes or comping stories you'd like to share with us, then please do send your contributions to me, Lynne Suzanne, at the address on page 100, stating whether you give permission for publication.

oooOOOooo

I am sure the advice in this book, *Win With Lynne - Simply Slogans,* will lead you along the road to continued success. Entering competitions is a wonderful hobby which offers the chance to visit interesting places and try out new experiences.

Even though compers are competing against each other, the friendship and fun is second to none. Should you decide to attend any of the nation-wide *Intacomps* Days, or a *Simply Slogans* weekend course, not only will you be able to pick up hints and tips but will make new comping friends, and for me, that's what makes it such a wonderful hobby.

May I wish you all success in the future. Best Wishes, **Lynne**

INDEX

Brainstorming	6, 11	**Tiebreakers, Styles of:**	
Courses, Simply Slogans weekends	36	Coined Words	56
Entry Form Services	87-89	Colours	56
Free-For-All	93	Comparisons	56
Info-finder	94-95	Compass	56
Intacomps	33-34, 41-42, 93, 95-97	Complements	57
Intacomps Days	36, 41	Contrast	57
Intaslogans	11-12, 27, 70, 93-94	Conversation	57
Phrases, Constructing	8, 21	Dialects	57
Prizewinning Slogans	70, 93	Environmental Issues	58
Reader's Features	89-93	Generations	58
Scansion	23	Inversion	58
Steps to Success	5-6	Involvement	59
Tiebreakers, Completing	5, 9, 23	In Words	59
Tiebreakers, Homonyms	45-46	Keep It Simple	59
Tiebreakers, Homophones	46-47	Limericks	59
Tiebreakers, Non-rhyming	24	Long Established	60
Tiebreakers, Perfecting	9, 27	Mathematics	60
Tiebreakers, Pink Carnations	43	Memories	60
Tiebreakers, Products:		Mottoes	60
Babycare	13, 71	Mouthwatering	60
Cleansers	13, 72	Names	61
Clothing	14, 73	Negatives	61
Confectionery	14, 74	Nostalgia	62
Cosmetics	15, 75	Numbers	62
Drinks, Alcoholic	15, 76	Partnerships	62
Drinks, Non Alcoholic	16, 76	Play on Words	8, 43
Electrical Appliances	16, 77	Please Please Take Me	63
Food, Bakery	17, 78	Praise	63
Food, Dairy	17, 79	Product Knowledge	64
Food, Fruit & Veg	17, 80	Problem Solving	64
Food, Meat	17, 81	Repetition	64
Laundry	18, 82	Sentiment	65
Tiebreakers, Rhyming	25-26	Sharing	65
Tiebreakers, Styles of:		Similarity	65
Abbreviations	48	Staccato	65
Acronyms	48	Sympathy	66
Adaptation	49-51	Topicality	66-67
Adverts	52	Trust	67
Alliteration	52	Value For Money	67
Amusing	53	Visit	67-69
Apt	53	Word Association	69
Chestnuts	54-55	Words Within Words	69

INDEX

Tiebreakers, Themes:		Travel, Countries:	
Motoring	18, 83	Africa & Middle East	20, 85
Sport:		Asia & Far East	20, 85
Cycling	19, 84	Australia	20, 85
Football	19, 84	Canada	20, 85
Golf	19, 84	Europe, France	20, 85
Horse Racing	19, 84	Europe, Germany	20, 85
Motor Racing	19, 84	Europe, Italy	20, 86
Olympic Events	19, 84	USA	20, 86
Skiing	19, 84	USA, California	86, 94-95
Snooker	19, 84	**Winn Sommor**	29, 36-41, 95-97
Tennis	19, 84	**Words of Phrase**	21

oooOOOooo

Titles from: L A Design Books

PO Box 11, Skegness, Lincs., PE25 3QH

Win With Lynne
How to Win Consumer Competitions
Lynne Suzanne
UK Price £15
0 9515011 2 7

Design And Cut
Flared Skirts
UK Price £9.95
0 9515011 3 5

Forthcoming title:

Win With Lynne
Winning Words
Lynne Suzanne
0 9515011 5 1

LYNFORMATION PACK

Win With Lynne
Simply Slogans

Lynformation Pack

An information pack containing details of:

Intacomps nationwide social days
Simply Slogans weekend courses
Intacomps quarterly newsletter
Free-For-All monthly booklet
Prizewinning Slogans
Intaslogans
Info-finder

Together with complimentary copies of:

Current month's Current Competition Update
Free-To-Enter Competition Update
Small batch of entry forms

Can be obtained by sending a stamped self addressed envelope to:

Lynne Suzanne's Information Pack
L A Design Books
Dept. WWLSS
PO Box 11
Skegness, Lincs.
PE25 3QH